Living the Simple Life

Also by Elaine St. James

SIMPLIFY YOUR LIFE

INNER SIMPLICITY

Living the Simple Life

A Guide to Scaling Down and Enjoying More

ELAINE ST. JAMES

HYPERION

New York

Designed by Nicola Ferguson

Library of Congress Cataloging-in-Publication Data

St. James, Elaine.

Living the simple life : a guide to scaling down and enjoying more /

Elaine St. James. — 1st ed.

p.   cm

ISBN: 0-7868-6219-X

1. Simplicity. 2. Conduct of life. 3. Spiritual Life. 4. St. James, Elaine.

I. Title

BJ1496.S73   1996

179' .9—dc20   96-3949

CIP

Paperback ISBN 0-7868-8242-5

First Paperback Edition

3   5   7   9   10   8   6   4

This book is dedicated to

everyone who wants to live a simpler life

ACKNOWLEDGMENTS

I am deeply indebted to Catha Paquette for her perceptive and insightful reading of the manuscript.

I'd like to thank Marcia Burtt, Joe Phillips, and Pat Rushton for their advice and assistance throughout the process of writing this book.

I'm grateful for the continuing friendship and support of Judy Babcock, Phil Babcock, Himilce Novas, Tiffany Miller, Marisa Kennedy Miller, Jackie Powers, Carolyn Howe, Meg Torbert, Bev Brennan, Vera Cole, and Jamie O'Toole, and for the presence and guidance of Michael Russer, Stu Sherman, Bob Maloy, Don Foster, Michelle Gysan, Colleen McCarthy Evans, and Maryke White.

I'd like to thank my agent, Jane Dystel, and my publisher, Bob Miller, for helping me put this book together, and I especially appreciate the wisdom, direction, and encouragement of my editor, Laurie Abkemeier.

Many thanks to Cynthia Ferguson, Carlie Gnatzig, Erin Webreck, and all the other readers who gave me permission to use their comments in this book, and to everyone who wrote to share their excitement, their enthusiasm, and their ideas for living simpler lives.

I thank my husband, Wolcott Gibbs, Jr., for everything, most especially for helping me keep life simple.

CONTENTS

Contents

Contents

FOUR   Some Things to Think About

Contents

Contents

Contents

Contents

Living the
Simple Life

AN OVERVIEW

I first made the decision to start living a simpler life in the summer of 1990. Prior to that time I had spent roughly twelve years as a real estate investor. I worked ten-hour days buying, refurbishing, managing, and selling investment properties.

During the previous year I had organized a real estate seminar business, had written a book on real estate investing, and had just completed a national media tour to promote it.

My life was ruled by a black leather time management system that weighed five pounds and took up half my desk space. My day was driven by the classic prioritizing question, "What is the best use of my time right now?"

Sometime after college I began, as many of us did, to work at two speeds: faster and fastest. I moved at this pace from six in the morning until seven or eight o'clock at night for more years than I care to count.

It would probably be accurate to say that I had become a fairly typical urban professional on my own fast track.

Though my husband, Gibbs, who is older and wiser than I am, was never technically a yuppie, his life was complicated by the fact that he was married to one. And he, too, maintained a full career schedule as a magazine editor, while at the same time writing a series of adventure novels. He was also an active volunteer with various community organizations.

In addition to our time-consuming careers, we had all the other duties and responsibilities associated with maintaining our lives. Though my two stepsons—who had been with us on weekends for the previous eight years—were now out on their own, we still had four cats and a busy social life.

The gods must have been smiling on me in the summer of 1990. I stopped for five minutes in the middle of July that year, and in a quiet moment I looked at my time management system as though I were seeing it for the first time. As I went over the list of phone calls I had to make, the people I had to see, the places I had to go, and the things I had to do, all of a sudden a light bulb went on. I realized my life had become too complicated, and I made the decision then and there to start simplifying it.

I had finally reached a point where keeping up such a hectic pace no longer seemed worth it. It occurred to me that we had, through long hours and a lot of hard work, achieved a modicum of success. We had many of the trappings of the modern lifestyle, but we didn't have the time, and sometimes not even the energy, to enjoy them. And even worse, we had little time for each other, and practically no time for ourselves.

A large part of the dissatisfaction for me was that I had never particularly enjoyed my work. I had continued to do it because I hadn't a clue what else I might be able to do. At that moment it was unthinkable that I could change my career or cut back on my work schedule.

But I decided there were many other areas where we could begin to cut back. My first objective was to create some breathing space so we could start to figure out how we could do things differently.

• • •

And so we began the process of simplifying. In the first couple of months we eliminated a lot of the clutter that was taking up our time and energy, and we moved to a smaller home. Over the next couple of years we made significant changes in our household routines, our social lives, our entertainment patterns, our civic and volunteer schedules, our financial picture, our personal lives, and eventually even our work lives.

I then got the idea to write a book on the things we had done to scale back. That book, *Simplify Your Life: 100 Ways to Slow Down and Enjoy the Things That Really Matter*, was published in May 1994. It outlines many of the steps Gibbs and I took to simplify.

In the process of simplifying the outer areas of our lives, we freed up close to thirty hours a week. This gave me the opportunity to begin the daunting prospect of thinking about making some career changes, and also the chance to address some of the emotional, psychological, and spiritual issues that had been bubbling beneath the surface of my fast-paced life, but that I'd seldom taken the time to explore.

I then decided to write a book that would discuss some of those issues. And so I wrote *Inner Simplicity: 100 Ways to Regain*

Peace and Nourish Your Soul, which was published in May 1995.

When we first made the decision to simplify, we had no idea that we were in the beginning phase of a major national trend. We simply wanted to get out from under the complications that twelve fast-paced years had generated.

If you, too, are thinking about making some changes and simplifying, or have already started the process, you're not alone.

According to the Trends Research Institute of Rhinebeck, New York, a privately funded organization that forecasts and tracks changes in our culture, simplifying is one of the leading movements of the decade.

A 1995 nationwide survey of a cross section of Americans revealed that close to 30 percent of the respondents had *voluntarily* downshifted, and were working fewer hours for less pay so they could spend more time with their families.

Numerous other surveys have shown that anywhere from 60 to 80 percent of those questioned would be willing to accept a reduction in pay if they could work fewer hours.

This represents a major nationwide change in personal priorities. It says that many of us have had enough of the fast-paced, hard-working lifestyle that has become "the norm" over the last decade. It says millions of Americans want to live their lives differently.

The Trends Institute estimates that by the end of the decade, a total of 15 percent of the 77 million baby boomers will have made significant moves toward creating simpler lives, some voluntarily, others involuntarily.

When I wrote *Simplify Your Life*, I thought I was writing it for *maturing* yuppies, who, like Gibbs and me, had been seduced by both the work and the consumer culture in recent years, and who in the process of overdoing it, had begun to lose sight of the important things.

But based on the letters I receive from readers around the country, it would appear that the desire to simplify crosses most generational, economic, educational, and professional lines.

I hear from teenagers, single men and women, married couples, retirees, the affluent, the not so affluent, and people from every walk of life—teachers, nurses, computer specialists, actors, journalists, artists, psychotherapists, legislators, lawyers, corporate executives, police officers, students, and media personalities. They are among the millions of Americans who are reducing, voluntarily or otherwise, the hours they spend earning a salary, their housing requirements, and the money they spend on goods and services.

They, like Gibbs and me, are realizing that they've given up too much in the effort to have it all. The primary objective for most of them is to have more time for their own life dreams or for the people they love, and for doing the things they really want to do.

When you stop to think about it, it's not surprising that so many of us want to simplify. Never before in the history of mankind have so many people been able to have so much, go so many places, and do so many things. We've worn ourselves out trying to have it all.

And now we're ready to look at other options.

In *Living the Simple Life*, we'll explore what simple living means to different people and look at what complicates our lives, what we can eliminate, and ways we can play the game differently (Chapter One). I'll outline some ways to get started, especially for those who feel their lives are too complicated to even think about simplifying (Chapter Two), and for those who may not have stopped long enough recently to get in touch with what really matters to them (Chapter Three).

I'll point out some of the things Gibbs and I have learned over the past few years about having more time to call our own, and suggest how to deal with people who don't understand the desire to simplify (Chapter Four).

In my experience two major issues complicate our lives above all else. The first is our ongoing battle with consumerism and the stuff we've accumulated. As with any problem, awareness is the first step toward resolution. And so I'll share what we've learned about letting go of a lot of that stuff, and some of the ways we've dealt with the media-generated imperative to consume (Chapters Five and Six).

The second challenge is the tendency for many of us to say yes when we'd like to say no, a habit that affects all areas of our lives. In Chapter Seven, I'll discuss ways we've used to approach this.

One of the great dichotomies we face is that because our lives are so complicated we don't have time for ourselves and at the same time we often keep our lives complicated so we won't have to address some of our inner issues. I'll talk about this and some ways we can bring our outer and inner lives together in Chapter Eight.

Each passing year leaves us with personal, household, and lifestyle choices that can either simplify our lives or complicate them even further. In Chapters Nine and Ten, I'll share my experiences—as well as some readers' ideas—about these choices.

There is perhaps no one for whom the problems of consumerism and learning to say no are more important or more challenging than for parents. In Chapter Eleven, I'll combine my own observations with the wisdom of several readers and an expert or two to outline some ideas for simplifying with children.

Having no options complicates our lives. Having too many options complicates our lives as well. In Chapter Twelve, I'll discuss some ways I've learned to deal with the clothing options for women. In Chapter Thirteen, Gibbs discusses some things he's always known about clothing options for men.

I've also included a Reading List, a selection of books that explores some more of the organizational, financial, lifestyle, and work-related questions of living a simpler life.

An interviewer asked me recently if I was glad I made all these changes and had simplified my life. I said I was, absolutely.

Then she asked if I'd do it again. I said yes, absolutely. There's no way I'd ever want my life to be so complicated again.

Then she asked if I would have simplified if someone else had suggested it to me—before I came to the decision on my own. My initial reply was, probably not!

But as I thought about it some more, I realized that if someone had outlined easy changes I could make which would free up some time without derailing the rest of my schedule, I believe I would have paused long enough to consider them.

If someone had been able to show me that just by tweaking my daily routine I would have more time each week—not to work more but to *play* more and *relax* more—I like to think I'd have been open to that possibility.

If someone had pointed out that *reducing* the hours I spend in the office each day could actually make me more productive, I would have been open to experimenting with that.

If I could have seen that freeing up more time for leisure would help open me up to my creativity, which in turn would make it possible for me to move away from a career I'd never been happy in and into one that now is a constant source of joy...Well, I might have been skeptical, but because hope springs eternal, I'd have sought out that leisure time.

And if someone had convinced me that eventually I could use some of my newfound time to face the more difficult challenges I'd spent years avoiding—such as conquering my fears and learning to forgive—and that doing those things in turn would free me for unprecedented personal and inner growth, I like to think I'd have gone for it.

So that's what I'd like to do for you in Living the Simple Life. If you're just starting to consider the possibility of simplifying, I want to give you a glimpse of the tremendous freedom you'll experience when you start to eliminate some of the day-to-day complexities.

You'll see that simplifying is not necessarily about getting rid of everything we've worked so hard for. It's about making wise choices among the things we now have to choose from. It's about recognizing that trying to have it all has gotten in the way of enjoying the things which do add to our happiness and well-being. So it's about deciding what's important to us, and grace-fully letting go of the things that aren't.

You'll see that simplifying is not necessarily about moving to Walden Pond and sending the laundry home to Mother. It's about simplifying our lives right where we are. It's about learn-ing to reduce the laundering chore, along with all the other chores and frequently self-imposed obligations, so we can begin to make the contributions we all, in our heart of hearts, want to make to our family, to our community, to our environment, and to the world.

If you've already begun taking steps to simplify, *Living the Sim-ple Life* will help you continue on your way, perhaps with some ideas you may not have thought of, and possibly with some dif-ferent ways of thinking about the process.

If you've long been living the simple life, I hope you'll find here some reinforcement and even validation for the sometimes easy, sometimes difficult, but almost always rewarding choices you've made.

When you start slowing down, cutting back, creating time— real time for yourself—the important things become obvious. Once you simplify your life you begin, perhaps again, to do your best work. You can start, perhaps all over again, to live your best life, whatever that is for you.

Simplifying is not a panacea. It won't solve all the problems of our lives or of the world. But it's a good beginning.

ONE

The Simple Life

1. What Living the Simple Life Means for Me and Gibbs

When my husband, Gibbs, and I first made the decision to simplify our lives in the summer of 1990, we weren't sure what living the simple life would mean for us. In many respects we had a good life; we just didn't have the time or the energy to enjoy it.

We knew we didn't want to drop out. We weren't ready to move to the woods. We didn't want to give *everything* away. We're too young to retire, and were not in a financial position to do so, anyway. Our challenge was to create a simpler life right where we were, in a town we love, with people we care about.

For us, simplifying meant, among other things, getting rid of an accumulation of possessions that were no longer adding anything to our lives and were taking up a lot of space in our closets and storage spaces. It was about moving to a smaller, easier-to-maintain home.

It was about cutting back on the daily and weekly household routines—cooking, grocery shopping, housecleaning, yard maintenance, errand running—and using the time we'd freed up to watch the sunset, or to putter in the rose garden, or to spend time with family and friends.

It was about changing our buying patterns, not only to reduce our consumption of the earth's resources, but also to minimize the stuff we have to take care of, insure, and provide space for.

It was about learning to say no to many of the social and civic activities we'd often felt obligated to do, so we'd have time to enjoy the silence, or start one of our creative projects, or learn to do nothing for a change.

For Gibbs, who loves his work, it was about eliminating a stressful three- to four-hour daily commute so his workday wasn't so exhausting and so we had more time together. He also wanted to have more time for his writing and to pursue his community and volunteer interests.

For me, it was about going from exhausting ten- and twelve-hour workdays in a career that never fed my soul to a six- to eight-hour day of writing that thrills me to the core.

It was about gradually, over the course of a couple of years, changing our daily routine so that, rather than having to rush mindlessly to begin our respective work schedules, we now have four uninterrupted hours to read, to contemplate, to take walks along the beach together, to chat on the phone with a friend, and possibly to romp with the dogs before we start our workday.

We're still in the early stages of simplifying, so we don't yet know all the benefits that will come from continuing to live the simple life. But we see this as a good start and a big improvement over the hectic lives we'd been living for too many years.

2. Some Other Views of the Simple Life

Keep in mind that simplification is all relative. For example, Oprah Winfrey simplified her life by unloading, via a charity auction, several thousand of the exquisite outfits she has worn on her daily television show for the past ten years, and by figuring out that she can turn off the ringer on her home phone so she doesn't have to take calls if she chooses not to.

Barbra Streisand simplified her life by getting rid of five of her seven houses and her Tiffany lamp collection.

For David, a 42-year-old teacher who told his story at a presentation I gave in San Diego, simplifying means keeping his possessions down to eight boxes of personal items and one lamp to read by.

David uses his master's degree in education to tutor the children of affluent families. He decided twenty years ago to limit his work schedule to two hours a day, four days a week, which provides him all the income he needs to maintain his simple life. A good deal of the rest of his time is spent doing volunteer work with underpriviledged kids.

For Ellen, a 41-year-old single attorney who wrote to me from the Northwest, simplifying is about selling her home and unloading her private practice so she can take time off to figure out what she wants to do next (which definitely won't involve law and most assuredly won't involve maintaining a huge house).

Based on the letters I get from readers of *Simplify Your Life* and *Inner Simplicity* and the stories I hear from people I talk with around the country—as well as on reports circulating in the media—simplifying means taking one or two or a combination of steps to reduce the stress that has become a permanent fixture in our lives.

Sometimes it means exploring new career options, sometimes it means quitting our jobs altogether, but almost always it means cutting back on our heavy work schedules.

Sometimes it means moving to a smaller home or moving across country, and sometimes it means simply living differently in the space we have.

Sometimes it means getting rid of everything, but more often it means merely cutting back on the amount of stuff we've accumulated, and changing our spending habits because we're finally learning that too much is too much.

And sometimes simplifying means searching for balance between our need for a satisfying career, our desire to spend time with our families, and the need to nourish our inner selves.

For most of us, simplifying is any one or a combination of steps we can take to get back in control of our lives.

3. A "Corporate Yuppie" Approach to Simplifying

Dear Elaine,

I enjoyed *Simplify Your Life* and wanted to respond. We, too, have made a drastic lifestyle change for the better. We were yuppies at major corporations and enjoyed the material things and the fast-paced life in Dallas, Texas.

Then the kids came. They are now 2 years old and 7 months old, and they keep me busy. I have no time for fussiness or complications. People ask me how I do it, and I reply, "Simplicity and organization." We moved to a rural area up north and look forward to raising our kids with values and a wholesome environment.

The first thing I did when we decided to simplify was to quit my job. That step in itself eliminated day-care and transportation hassles. I'm trying to get another career going from my home.

I've always been a minimalist, but I really kicked into high gear after the kids came along.

I do a lot of the things your book mentions. I feel so free from our past stresses. The thing that makes me happiest is that I'm only 31 years old and learned this early in the game.

The hardest thing is trying to explain our lifestyle to people my age because they think our downscaling was motivated by a negative, such as my quitting my job, or because we can't afford things. It's the opposite, but people don't get it. We don't *want* an answering machine or call waiting. It's not that we can't afford it. Like you, I was constantly on the phone on my last job, and am not fond of the phone.

I've stopped trying to explain to people. Now I let them wonder why I'm so happy and secure in myself these days.

Sincerely,

Cynthia Ferguson

Byron Center, MI

4. A "Cabin in the Woods" Approach to Simple Living

Dear Elaine,

I live in Skagway, Alaska, ninety miles north of Juneau. Your book *Simplify Your Life* made it to my morning "wake up slowly time" (by reading a book and sipping warm apple cider) just this morning. It was a gift from relatives in Vail, Colorado. I had been feeling complicated and rushed lately, and decided to see what you had for me!

Soon, with a big smile, I realized that I had actually graduated from most of the one hundred simplifiers. Thank you for reminding me how most Americans live a crazy busy life compared to mine.

As I looked around my one-room cabin, taking in all 400 square feet of it, I laughed at myself for thinking my life was too complex. I live eight miles out of Skagway (population 720) in my cabin that has no electricity or running water other than the mountain creek that "runs" by my cabin that I've been drinking from for over five years. I have wood heat, a propane stove, and a neat and clean outhouse. I use the creek for refrigeration in summer, and a window box for a fridge in the winter. I can look out my window and see the harbor seals playing and hear the dolphins exhaling out of their blowholes.

For exercise, I chop all my own wood to burn and bike the eight miles to work most days of the week. In winter there are no open businesses in town to use me as their bookkeeper, so I have about five or six months off a year.

My quality of life is fantastic. Yesterday I saw both a bear and a coyote in my neighborhood. The eagle on the front of this card follows me to work in the mornings! I have clean air, clean water, and many loving friends who all live as simply as I do. I actually forget that most people don't live like me and my neighbors.

We aren't hippies or revolutionists. We simply simplified. You'd be amazed how much you can really pare down. I have hauled up a car battery that I run my radio/CD player on, but imagine how much space you'd have without all of your plug-in gadgets! Sometimes we rent movies and watch them at the public library. But the TV was the first thing I was delighted to part with.

Thank you for making your great ideas feasible for people who would not be able to make such a big step over to my lifestyle—but perhaps they'd be able to fire their personal trainer, or simplify their diet, or just smile at their neighbor.

Have a great day.

Carlie Gnatzig

Skagway, AK

5. What Does Simple Living Mean to You?

The levels of stress many of us have experienced in our fast-paced lifestyles have made us long for respite from the pressures of the modern world. The temptation is strong to think that respite would come from packing up and leaving it all behind.

But as Carlie Gnatzig points out, moving to a cabin in the woods is a big leap. Many people have left everything behind to move to the country, and then found that it's not necessarily simple or suitable.

Tempting as it might be to some, escaping to the woods is not the only way one can live a simple life. And it's probably not a realistic option for most of us.

And it's not necessary to make such sweeping changes in order to simplify, at least not to begin with. For many, even minor alterations to the lifestyle we're now living can bring significant relief.

The Simple Life

So before you order up the proper attire from L. L. Bean, you may find it helpful, if you haven't done so already, to take some time to figure out what simple living really means to you.

What do you hope to achieve by making some changes that would simplify your life? What would have to happen for you to live more simply? And how will you know when you've gotten there? Can you make some easy changes right where you are? Or would you have to move across town, or possibly across country to get to simple?

It's possible your ideas about simplifying will change as you go along. Keep in mind that what may be simple for someone else may not be simple for you. You may end up with an entirely different understanding of simple living than the one you start out with.

But it's so much easier to reach our destination when we at least have an idea of where it is we want to go.

6. The Things That Complicate Our Lives

Many things make life complicated for us. Here is a list of one hundred of them:

Big houses. Big mortgages. High-maintenance automobiles. Property taxes. Home remodeling. Inflation. Revolving charge accounts. Easy credit. Multiple credit cards. Credit card debt. Consumer debt. The national debt.

Not having time to spend with our spouses. Not having time to spend with our children. Difficult spouses. Children who are difficult because we don't have enough time to spend with them. Ex-spouses. Family obligations. Ailing parents. Step-parents. Uncooperative siblings. Stepchildren. Difficult in-laws. Family expectations. Our own expectations.

Fifty-hour work weeks. Sixty-hour work weeks. Having to hold down two jobs to meet the big mortgage payments and the multiple car payments. Long commutes. Heavy traffic. Traffic jams. Traffic accidents. Difficult bosses. Obstinate employees. Grudging co-workers. Demanding clients. Irksome partners. Silent partners who won't remain silent. Staff meetings. Breakdowns in communication. Work we don't particularly enjoy. Work we actively dislike. Working too many long hours, even if it's work we love. Unemployment.

Not having time to spend with friends. Not having time to spend alone. Pressing civic obligations. Committee meetings. Social commitments. Noisy neighbors. Incompetent physicians. Politics. Equivocating politicians. Congress. Attorneys. Lawsuits. Delivery people who show up a day late. Repairpeople who never show up. Contractors we wish had never shown up.

Publisher's Clearing House mailings. Unrelenting charity requests. Television. Advertising. Televised court proceedings. Telephone solicitors. Call waiting. The Net. E-mail. Registered mail. Junk mail.

Having too much stuff. Having no options. Having unlimited options. Planned obsolescence.

Alcohol. Drugs. Cigarettes. Pollution. Taxes. Unsafe sex. Dieting. Health fads. Exercise equipment we don't use. Over-the-counter medications that don't work. Cheap gadgets that don't work. Expensive gadgets that don't work. Relationships that don't work. Prescription medications that may solve one problem while creating another. Illness. Choosing an HMO.

Anger. Worry. Fear. Negative cash flow. Bad weather. Natural disasters. Inadequate day-care arrangements. Plastic grocery store baggies that don't open. Tax returns. Blown-in subscription cards.

Not necessarily in this order.

7. What We Can Eliminate

Not all of the previously mentioned things complicate life for all of us all of the time. But a lot of them make life difficult, sometimes more often than we're aware of.

In this culture, at this point in time, most of us won't be able to avoid all complications completely. But we can eliminate more than we think we can. We just have to learn to be selective.

And that's a big part of what simplifying is all about.

Reread the list of things that complicates our lives and mark any that apply to your life at the moment. If you think of any other things, add them to the list.

In this list there are less than a dozen that we probably won't be able to do anything about—not in this lifetime and not legally. They include inflation, the national debt, politics, attorneys, Publisher's Clearing House mailings, planned obsolescence, taxes, bad weather, natural disasters, and blown-in subscription cards.

Everything else on the list, and probably most of the items you may have added, we can either do something about or selectively avoid in one way or another.

Recognizing this will simplify your life. The rest is just details.

8. Remember a Time When You Were Truly Happy

Ask anyone who is past the age of 35 to recall a time when they were truly happy. Most people will say they're pretty happy now, though they may admit they sometimes feel overwhelmed by the demands of life these days.

If you press them further, a lot of people will remember a time in their youth, perhaps a particularly wonderful summer when they had few cares or responsibilities and spent seemingly endless weeks fishing on a quiet stream or lazing by the neighborhood pool.

Or perhaps they'll remember the joy of being young and single, or of being newly married and madly in love. They had few possessions to weigh them down, no house payment, maybe only a small car payment. They worked hard, but work didn't consume all their time and energy. Mostly they didn't worry about health insurance, life insurance, home insurance, interest rates, the Dow, or taxes. Life was simple.

Most of us wouldn't go back to being young and totally independent and having nothing at all to call our own. But many of us would like to recapture the *feeling* of those carefree days.

And sometimes, in the midst of simplifying, things can get overwhelming. If you're changing jobs, reducing your income, letting go of the clutter, cleaning up relationships, dealing with some of the inner issues, or changing your long-established habit patterns, life can, in the short term, seem pretty complicated.

So reconstruct your fond memories of happy, simpler times. Let them help create a clear picture of what simple living means for you. It will stand as a beacon for you in the process of getting back to the simple life.

9. Be Willing to Change the Way You Play the Game

Often one of the stumbling blocks to living a simpler life is our inability or unwillingness to change how we play some of the games that got us into these complicated lives in the first place.

For example, for many years I was driven by the "need" to maintain our home to certain standards of cleanliness, organization, efficiency, and so-called style. After we'd taken some of our first steps toward simplifying, such as moving to the smaller place and changing a lot of our buying patterns, I realized this was one area in which I wanted to make some significant changes.

When the town we live in was considering rationing water because of severe drought conditions, we made the decision to cut back on the amount of laundry we wash. This meant wearing our clothes a bit longer than we'd been used to, and not changing the sheets and towels every week as I'd always done.

To my surprise, I didn't have a problem with wearing our clothes longer between washings. Gibbs was once editor of *Yachting* magazine, so we've spent a lot of time on boats over the years and learned how to stand downwind from people!

But I grew up, as many of us did, in a household where we changed the sheets and towels every single week no matter what, so I had some difficulty reducing the frequency with which we laundered the linens.

Fortunately, my younger stepson, Eric, who had recently graduated from college, gave me some sage advice. He said, "Elaine, relax. I went for four years without changing the sheets."

The drought forced us to change the way we had always done the laundering chore. But Eric's comment helped me put things in perspective, and I began to see how approaching that weekly task differently had simplified our lives.

Gradually, I started to change some of my other expectations, such as how spotless my glasswear was or how clean my floors had to be. I began to look carefully at some of the routine household chores I'd always considered sacrosanct, such as the idea that our clothes have to be whiter than white, that our blues have to be bluer than blue, that our mirrors have to shine with a brilliant luster, or that our hardwood tabletops have to be polished to a blinding brightness.

When you examine these precepts closely you begin to see how absurd they are. Has anyone ever been fired for having a ring around the inside of a shirt collar? Is our spaghetti bolognese less delectable because we can't see our reflection off the side of the pan? Would houseguests actually leave, never to return again, if we didn't use fabric softener on our bath towels?

This is not to suggest that we eliminate housecleaning or laundry routines altogether, but simply that it's possible to think of doing them differently, or that we can set our own standards rather than dutifully accepting those advertised by cleaning product manufacturers.

Few of these dictates were determined by actual need, or even by our desires. They were set in the boardrooms of UniLever,

Bristol Myers/Squibb, and Johnson Wax, among others. Many dollars are spent each year to get us to accept these and countless other ideals as our own. We've been made to feel inadequate, incompetent, insecure, dissatisfied, and socially unacceptable if we don't meet them at every level.

In the last thirty years we've given up time with our families, our leisure time, our sleep time, our money, our rapidly depleting energy, and our own free choice in varying attempts to maintain many of these conventions. In doing so we have generously lined the pockets of a couple hundred corporate executives while vastly complicating our own lives.

Household cleaning routines are only one area in which we've abandoned our freedom of choice to the strategies of marketing gurus. Few areas of our lives are untouched by products that are designed for the sole purpose of getting us to feel insecure enough to part with our money. Our tastes in clothing, personal hygiene, health care, food, travel, automobiles, children's toys, and practically everything else is manipulated by the pronouncements of those cunning advertising demons.

I don't claim to have been able to free myself completely from all of these mostly preposterous decrees. Far from it. I'm still emotionally attached to my BMW, and it's unlikely I'll ever be able to let go of my Revlon-generated need for lipstick. But becoming aware of the origin of a lot of these attachments has made it possible for me to simplify in many other areas.

It's sometimes difficult to know where to draw the line. But as you start to think about ways you could simplify, become mindful of the number of things you do each day because of standards that were set in a marketing session at Procter & Gamble.

10. You *Can* Have a Simpler Job

For many of us, our jobs and our work schedules have been one of the major complications of our lives. Our material well-being depends on our paycheck. Without our monthly income how could we eat or make the mortgage or the car payments? Without our jobs, the whole house of cards would come tumbling down. Often our very identity depends on our being employed.

And so I often hear people say, "I can't simplify my life as long as I've got to make a living."

But if you've got a demanding, time-consuming job, that alone might be sufficient reason to simplify your life.

As we've seen, many people have already made changes in their lifestyle or are thinking about the possibility of downshifting, or possibly changing their career path altogether so they can free up time to spend with their families, or to create more leisure time.

According to a survey conducted by the Merck Family Fund, 28 percent of working adults said they had voluntarily reduced their income in the last five years because of changes in their priorities. Others are being forced to make such changes due to corporate downsizing and changes in the economy.

But if you're like I was a few years back, you may not be open to the possibility of making career changes right now. You could well be thinking, as I did, "You gotta be kidding. There's no way I could quit my job. And I could certainly never work part time. How could I support or help support my lifestyle if I did? I've got to make a living."

And, most likely, at this moment it's true: You can't quit your job. Not today. Not tomorrow. Maybe not next month. Maybe not even next year.

Once I could see my way clear to simplifying my life, it was not that big a step to begin cutting my workday back to eight or nine hours. But it was several years before I could seriously think about unloading the real estate and doing something else. In the midst of a complicated life, it often is impossible to change jobs, or even to think about it.

So if the thought of making changes in your job picture presses all your buttons, don't even think about it now. Instead, look at all the other areas of your life you can simplify.

Simplifying in other areas will give you some breathing room. It'll give you more time. It'll give you more energy. It will reduce many of the financial pressures—if you're living more simply, you'll simply be spending less money.

Having more time and less stress will open your mind to possibilities you may not even be able to think about now. And eventually, as you pare away all the extraneous stuff, a new way of approaching your present job or an entirely different career option may be staring you in the face.

Yes, most of us have to make a living. And we have to look at ways we can support ourselves not only now, but throughout our retirement years. But if Vicki Robin and Joe Dominguez, authors of *Your Money or Your Life*, have been able to live on $500 a month for the past twenty years, then many things are possible in terms of career and employment changes for all of us.

This doesn't mean we all can live on $500 a month, but it

shows us that it is possible to live, and live well and happily, on a lot less than we've led ourselves to believe.

By slowing down, by simplifying, by breaking some of our consuming and spending habits, by teaching our kids simple pleasures, and by adopting simple pleasures ourselves, we can create a beautiful, happy, fulfilling life. And we won't have to work as hard as we have been to maintain it.

11. You Can Live a Simpler Life

I spoke to a bookstore owner recently who described people's reactions when they came up to the cash register with their books and saw a copy of *Simplify Your Life* sitting in a stack on the counter. Time and again he saw people pick up the book and read the title. And then they'd laugh. He said they laughed right out loud because the idea that anyone could actually simplify his or her life in this day and age seemed so preposterous.

But, while waiting for their purchases to be totaled up, they'd flip through the book, just out of curiosity.

Then they'd say, "Ah, yes, if I dropped call waiting, that would simplify my life."

Or, "Yes, if I didn't have to answer the phone every time it rings, that would simplify my life."

Or, "Yes, if I started doing just one thing at a time, that would simplify my life. And if I cleaned up my relationships, that would *really* simplify my life."

And they began to get the idea that there *are* things we can do to simplify. Easy things—like leaving our shoes at the front door or changing the way we do the holidays—that would make a difference.

They also see there are other steps—like changing our expectations, or learning to forgive, or getting out of debt—that are more difficult perhaps, but are possible, and that would significantly reduce the complexity of our lives.

But I understand the initial skepticism. At first glance, the idea of creating a simple life often seems out of the question.

When we're in the midst of a complicated life, we think it would be impossible to slow down. When we're constantly racing against the clock, it feels like there's no way to create some extra time. When we're so exhausted from moving ninety miles an hour, we're certain we don't have the energy to figure out how to do things differently.

When we're torn between the pressures of work, the demands of our children, and the needs of our inner selves, it feels as though there's no way we could add one more thing, like simplifying, to our list of things to do.

But it is possible. And there's a magical, almost exponential quality about time. Once you free up even a little bit of it, other ways will start occurring to you to help free up even more.

If you don't know where to begin, start with one of the easy steps outlined in the next chapter.

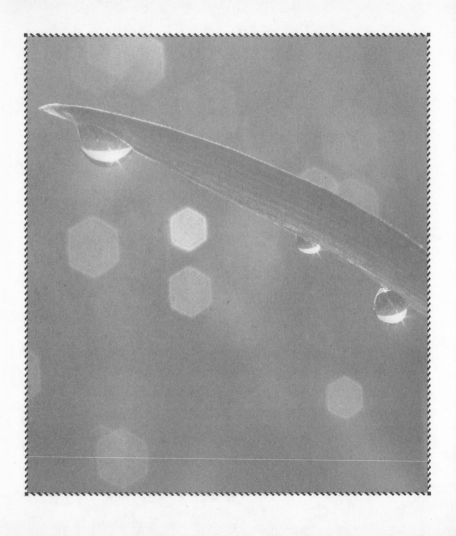

TWO

Getting Started

12. A First Step

People frequently ask me, "How can I possibly simplify my life? I'm working too hard. I'm moving too fast. I've got my career, my marriage, the kids, the mortgage payment, and the car payments to think about. My life is too complicated for me to take the time to stop and simplify."

I know exactly what they mean. My life was that complicated a few years back. Even if I could stop for a bit, I felt I wouldn't know where to begin. But finally, as many of us have, I reached the point of desperation. I had to start making some changes, and begin to simplify my life.

But it didn't happen overnight. It took us several years of concerted effort to create a simpler life.

This is not to say that everything we did to simplify was difficult. Far from it. There were many things—like changing our exercise regimen, spending more time in nature, and creating time for solitude—that were relatively easy and gave us immediate relief.

But if you've been living what we have come to think of as a normal life in this culture, it's unreasonable to expect that you can simplify your entire life this Saturday between noon and 3 p.m. Realistically, it's just not going to happen.

Simplifying is a process. It no doubt took you years to build your complicated, high-pressure life. It will take some time to simplify it. You can't undo it all today. But you can get started today.

To start simplifying the only thing you have to do right now is decide that you really want to simplify, and then schedule some time to think about it. That's it. Making that decision and setting aside the time is enough for one day.

How much time do you need to schedule? It depends to some extent on how complicated your life is and how adept you are at changing gears. When I decided to simplify, I scheduled a four-day weekend at a local retreat house. It took a day and a half for me to unwind enough just to get to the point where I could begin to think clearly about my life. If you mull it over for a few minutes, you'll know whether you can get started in an afternoon, or whether you need a couple of days or more.

A weekend provides a reasonable amount of time for most people. If you have a very complicated life, you may need that much time just to get into the process.

If you feel you can't take the whole weekend right now, take half of it. If you can't spend a whole day, then take half a day.

In the next week, just schedule whatever time you think it'll take. That's the first step.

Don't underestimate the tremendous power of taking a simple step like this. An amazing thing starts to happen when you begin to simplify your life: Each step you take will make it easier for you to take the next step. I promise you, if you make the decision to simplify, and commit to it, incredible things will happen.

13. Ten Ways to Free Up an Hour or More Each Day for the Next Thirty Days, So You Can Start Thinking about How to Simplify Your Life

If you feel your schedule is so jammed that you don't see how you could slow down enough to even begin thinking about simplifying, take a few moments to consider some of the suggestions here.

This is a list of reasonably painless ways to free up an hour or more each day—that's ten to twenty hours each week—for the next month.

For right now, you don't have to think of these as long-term changes—or as something you'll have to do forever in order to create more time for yourself—although you may ultimately want to incorporate many of them into your simple life.

There may only be a couple of ideas that apply to your life at the moment. Pick one (or two or more) that will work for you, and stick with it for thirty days:

1. If your job allows, quit work an hour earlier than you usually do and use that time to think about your life.

2. If your job allows, start work an hour later than you usually do and use the quiet time at home—after everyone else has gone—to think about your life.

3. If possible, stay at your office an hour later than you usually do, and use the time to think about your life. Do this only if you can be certain you will have uninterrupted time there.

4. Get up an hour earlier. This may also mean you go to bed an hour earlier; but an hour in the morning when you're rested and refreshed is worth two hours at the end of the day when you're exhausted.

5. Stop watching TV news.

6. Stop watching TV (period). Unplug it and move it to an out-of-the-way spot if necessary. Do this even if

you believe watching television relaxes you. It may, but it also programs you—in ways we're often not even conscious of—to continue to complicate your life. And it clutters up your mind with distractions that keep you feeling overwhelmed.

7. Don't schedule any lunch dates.

8. Don't schedule any after-work social hours. No coffees. No pre-dinner drinks. No dinners. No after-dinner drinks.

9. Stop reading the daily newspaper. (It's only for a month!)

10. Change your exercise regimen. For example, cut your daily program in half. Or, if you commute to a gym or an aerobics class, exercise at home and save the commute time. Or exercise just two or three days a week. Be creative here; it's only for thirty days.

14. Ten Ways to Free Up Miscellaneous Amounts of Time over the Next Thirty Days, So You Can Start Thinking about How to Simplify Your Life

Many of these ideas are not only about freeing up time, they're also about reducing the physical, mental, and emotional static that constantly occupies our minds, drains our energy, and keeps us from being in touch with how we would live our lives if we didn't have so many distractions.

1. Plan to stay off the phone, except for business or for emergencies. Announce to family and friends that you won't be chatting on the phone for the next month. (You might be astounded at how much time you save and how much internal noise you eliminate each day by cutting back on your social phone calls.)

2. Stop listening to the radio, the CD player, and your Walkman—at home, in the car, at the office, when you exercise.

3. Stop reading magazines. Recycle or pass on to a friend the stack of magazines sitting on your reading table waiting for you to find the time to read them.

   Do the same with any magazines that arrive in the mail during the next month. Don't set them aside and think you'll read them when the month is up. If you do that, you'll be just as behind then as you are now. You have to start someplace.

4. Stop all escape-type reading—detective stories, murder mysteries, fantasies.

5. Simplify your family meals as much as possible. Plan to prepare batches of soups or casseroles ahead of time and freeze them in serving portions. Or buy a month's supply of frozen dinners. (It's only for a month.) Make sure there is plenty of fresh fruit available. Dr. Spock always said if kids have fruit, they don't have to eat their vegetables. Use paper plates to minimize cleanup.

Enlist the help of your mate and children in the preparation, provisioning, and cleanup of meals, including breakfasts and lunches. Make a game out of this for your kids. Make a challenge out of this for your spouse.

6. Do only the minimal housekeeping chores. Keep the house picked up and orderly, but don't worry about dusting, vacuuming, window washing, mowing the lawn, waxing the car, or polishing the candelabrum.

You may have to change your expectations about how clean your house has to be to do this. Or you may have to change the expectations your mate or your mother or Madison Avenue has laid on you (#9).

7. Do minimal laundry. Our mothers did the week's laundry for the entire family in one day or less, without the high-tech machinery we have today. I know women who now wash a load or two every night of the week.

If we learn to be careful about how we wear our clothes—and train our kids to be careful, too—we can greatly reduce the laundering chore, at least for a month.

We can let the sheets and towels go for a week or more.

Make a quick calculation right now as to how much time you'd save you if you allowed yourself to do the laundry differently. How many evenings would it free up? How much of the weekend?

8. With the exception of groceries, eliminate all shopping. Stock up on things you might need ahead of time. Or simply do without. No one has ever died from running out of eye shadow. Or shaving cream.

Think of this as a personal challenge, and be prepared to use some of your self-discipline. The urge to rush out and buy something we think we need has become overwhelming in this culture. Multibillion-dollar media campaigns ensure that this urge continues. You'll be amazed at how much time you'll save when you learn to break this habit.

9. Don't accept or arrange any social or family engagements.

10. Cancel all civic or volunteer obligations. Simply say, "Sorry, but I'm starting a new project and won't have time for anything for thirty days."

Take five minutes right now to see if there are any other things particular to your schedule and lifestyle that you could change or eliminate to free up some time over the next thirty days.

Obviously you can extend any of these ideas into a 60- or a 90- or a 365-day plan. The idea is to free up as much of your time as possible so you can start thinking about some long-term changes you can make in your life.

15. Five Ways to Free Up an Entire Day or More over the Next Thirty Days, So You Can Start Thinking about How to Simplify Your Life

1. Take vacation days on Mondays or Fridays to give yourself a couple of three-day weekends. Or take some stand-alone vacation days in the middle of the week.
2. Take a week or more of vacation time, and use it to get started simplifying your life.
3. Take a couple of sick days or personal days.
4. Make an arrangement with your boss to work four ten-hour days for the next month (or permanently), and use the fifth day each week to start simplifying.
5. Plan to spend a Saturday or a Sunday or an entire weekend at home with no social or family commitments (except for your immediate family). Remember to eliminate the standard distractions, such as the radio and television, during this time.

16. Escape to a Quiet Spot

No doubt some people can arrange quiet time at home and actually make progress there in these first few steps.

But if your life is anything like mine was, you've got so much going on at home that you wouldn't be able to have an extended period of time without interruptions. Therefore, it might be easier if you can get away from your home or work environment.

This includes being away from phones, faxes, radios, television, the fridge, laundry, friends, neighbors, bosses, co-workers, and all other potential preoccupations.

One of your best options for an extended period of undisturbed time would be a nearby monastery or retreat house where you'll have a simple but comfortable room without a phone—where meals are included, and the entire atmosphere is arranged for a contemplative withdrawal from the world. (Check out *Sanctuaries*, by Jack and Marcia Kelley.)

As an alternative, consider renting a convenient motel room for a couple of days, and give out the phone number only for use in emergencies.

Spend some time right now thinking about the ideal place that would suit your circumstances.

Maybe you have friends who will be away on vacation and would be open to having you use their space for a couple of days.

Or perhaps you know someone who has a summer home or a cabin in the woods that you could rent or borrow for the time you need.

Or if you're comfortable with roughing it, get out your camping gear and head for the hills.

If you can't get away from home for a couple of days right now, but can see your way clear to freeing up an hour or so every morning, consider finding a quiet table at your local library, or an empty pew in a church, as a place in which to get started thinking about your life.

Another alternative is the great outdoors, perhaps on a park bench.

If you simply can't get away from your home, then do what you can to create the time and space there for quiet contemplation without the usual interruptions. Unplug the phone, turn off the radio and the TV, cancel your coffee break with your next-door neighbor.

If you're a mother with young children, hire a babysitter for a couple of afternoons. Or find a friend who wants to simplify, too—or who at least is sympathetic to your desire to simplify—and trade babysitting for a couple of afternoons or evenings.

Do whatever you need to do to find a space that will work for you. And do what you can to make it special. It's possible that this time will be for you, as it was for me, a major turning point in the way you live your life. It will be fun for you to be able to look back on this time and space fondly, and with sweet memories.

17. What to Take with You

This might seem like a minor point, but for those of us who are addicted to our stuff, it will serve as a helpful reminder.

To some people it's probably obvious that if you're going to hole up for a couple of days away from home with the purpose of thinking about simplifying your life, you'll want to take only a minimum amount of paraphernalia. However, it wasn't apparent to me when I left for my retreat, so I'll mention it here.

When I headed off to the hermitage for a mere four days, I had two satchels packed with personal belongings. One was full of clothes, shoes, and other personal items I didn't need and, in fact, most of which I never used. The other was loaded with books, magazines, notebooks, paper, pens, tapes and a tape player, and other miscellaneous stuff—most of which I also never used but had included on the "you never know when you might need it" theory.

I lugged all this baggage up a couple of flights of stairs and into my simple room, which was suddenly no longer quite so simple. After sorting through it all, I realized there was more than I'd actually use. Since it was getting in my way, I packed some of it up and took it back down to the car.

When I set out on similar missions these days—which I do on a regular basis—I leave the books and the tapes behind. I take a change of clothes, a toothbrush, a pen, and a notebook. When I thought about it later, I realized that's all I actually used, though I spent a fair amount of time and energy being preoccupied with all the other things.

This is a microcosm of the macrocosm for a lot of us in this culture: We're continually overwhelmed with and distracted by our stuff.

You might want to keep this in mind if you're packing for a brief retreat from the world.

18. Ask Yourself Some Simple Questions

Once you've created the time and have found a quiet place in which to think, a powerful next step is to ask yourself some simple questions.

One of the most obvious things to ask is "What is complicating my life right now?" Is it career pressures? Your relationship with your boss? With your co-workers? Are you spending too much time working? Too much time commuting? How could you cut back in these areas?

Sometimes simply taking the time to pinpoint the hot spots can go a long way toward alleviating the pressure.

The next obvious question to ask yourself would be "What do I need to do to simplify these areas?"

No one knows the minute details of your day or the secret wishes of your psyche better than you do. No one knows the answers to these questions better than you do, either.

Of course, your life may have become so complicated that even you are momentarily out of touch with the innermost workings of your being.

So getting to the point where you can ask the questions could be the easy part. Waiting for the answers can be the hard part. You may have to be patient. You'll definitely have to cut back on the distractions to listen carefully.

One of your toughest tasks may be forcing yourself to pay attention to the answer. You may be hearing things you don't want to hear. Your inner voice may be telling you that what you need to do is to quit your job or to find a new career or to move on from a relationship that isn't working. Remember, one of the reasons we keep our lives complicated is so we won't have to listen to our inner voice telling us what we need to do to make our lives work better.

But asking these questions can start the ball rolling. Keep a journal or notebook handy and write down any thoughts, insights, or solutions that come to you.

Even now, several years later, I've found it helpful to keep these questions in mind if I notice my life starting to get complicated again.

19. Set Your Own Pace

I've heard from many people who quit their jobs, left their mates, moved across country, and virtually started their lives over, all in one fell swoop.

But there are many for whom that drastic approach would be neither comfortable nor appropriate.

Where you start and how quickly you move along will depend to some extent on where you're at in your life right now, as well as on the type of person you are.

Obviously, there is no right or wrong way to begin the process of simplifying. If giant steps work for you, take them.

If you're not sure where to begin, creating the time to think about your life would probably be essential. Where you go from there and how quickly you do it will be up to you.

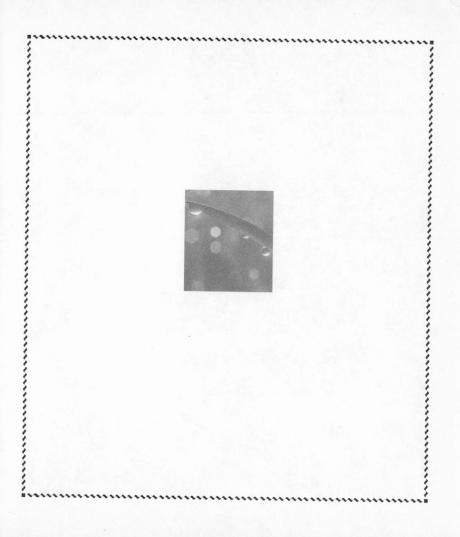

THREE

The Things That Really Matter

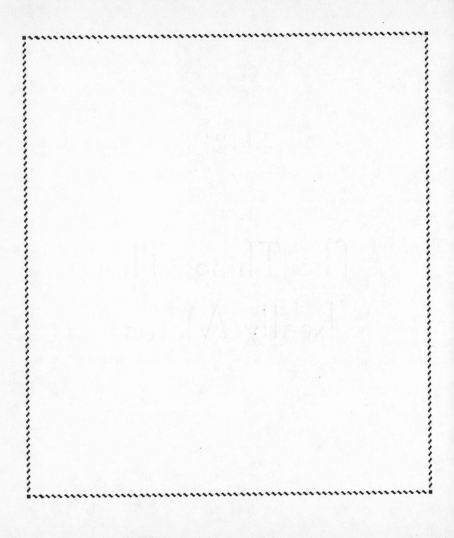

20. You May Not Know What Really Matters

According to a recent TIME/CNN poll, close to 65 percent of us spend much of our so-called leisure time doing things we'd rather not do. That is a staggering statistic, especially when you consider the incredible number of options that are available to us today.

I think there are two reasons a lot of us aren't doing the things we really want to do. First of all, many us don't know what those things are.

When I think back to my hectic lifestyle, I have to admit that one of the reasons I allowed my life to continue to be so complicated is that I hadn't slowed down enough in recent years to figure out what I wanted to do, not only in terms of my work life, but in terms of a lot of my personal choices.

I knew the basic things: I knew that Gibbs, and family, and special friends were important. I knew that for me, spending time in nature was important. I knew maintaining my health with exercise and an appropriate diet were important.

But there were other areas, such as my life's work and many social and leisure activities, I just sort of drifted along with because it was easier than taking the time to come up with alternatives.

For any number of reasons we lose sight of what we want to do. Perhaps we weren't encouraged as children to make our own decisions.

Or maybe we have easygoing, compliant personalities and have gone along with what other people have wanted to do, or wanted us to do, for so long that we've forgotten what's important to us.

Or perhaps we never allowed ourselves to believe that doing the things we enjoy is even a possibility for us.

If you've spent a lot of years not knowing what you really want to do, either in terms of your career or in terms of your personal, social, civic, or family life, it can seem like an impossible task to stop what you've been doing—or at least slow down for a bit—and figure it out. It often seems easier to keep on doing things we don't want to do.

Secondly, what we want to do can often be difficult to do.

For example, if your deep, dark, hidden desire is to write the great American novel, it would seemingly require a major disruption in your life to arrange things so you could even get started on it. Often it's easier to continue doing things you almost want to do, or don't mind doing.

So our lives get frittered away by a social engagement here, a luncheon there, an evening of television here, or the habit of working evenings or weekends or both on projects that we don't have all that much interest in. And the things we really want to do, in our heart of hearts, get put on the back burner.

One of the things simplifying your life will do is free up time for you to figure out what really matters to you, and then enable you to arrange your time so you can do it.

21. Reexamine Your List of Goals

Not being clear on what I wanted to do didn't keep me from having lots of lists of things I *thought* I wanted to do. Paradoxically, it may have contributed to the length of my lists.

When I made the decision to simplify my life, I had a full-sized three-ring binder time management system in which I had a goals page for each of the major areas of my life, including personal, career, social, financial, spiritual, and civic. In each of these categories I had a to-do list that included projects I thought I wanted to start.

For example, my personal list included the following projects, among others:

Start painting

Start drawing

Study landscape gardening

Learn to write

Join a choral group/study voice

Learn Spanish. Brush up on French and German.

Learn speed reading.

Learn flower arranging, especially Ikebana

Study art history

Start bird watching

Study the Middle East situation in depth

Get into hang gliding

Start writing letters

Study screenwriting

Study filmmaking

Learn Beethoven's *Moonlight Sonata* for Christmas recital

Become a gourmet cook (!)

Learn the basics of interior design

Learn about growing roses

Start mountain hiking

This time management system also included the following: time lines with starting and completion dates and to-do sheets for each of the items within the above mentioned categories; a mission statement; a purpose statement; and a three-page constantly expanding reading list. It also, of course, had a two-page spread for every day of the year on which were outlined the activities connected with my daily schedule.

Obviously, if I was going to simplify my life, one of the first things I was going to have to do was to reconsider my goals.

Though it's difficult for me to believe this now, before I simplified my life I was committed to the idea that I'd eventually—and sooner rather than later—be able to do all the things I had on these lists.

If you'd asked me at that time what really matters, I'd have insisted that it all mattered. It never occurred to me to give up any of it.

I look at this list now and I can laugh. The only reason I have the courage to reveal the absurdity of these lists is that now I know I was not alone. There are millions of other people out there who believe, as I did, that we can do it all, have it all, be it all. Or at least do most of it; and who perhaps even yet are carrying around similar lists—comparable in scope if not in content—in their leather-bound time management systems.

I know that keeping lists can be beneficial in terms of helping us figure out what's important. But if, as many of us did, you got carried away with your lists, you may have to reconsider and cut your lists back to more realistic proportions.

I found this to be an ongoing process that unfolded over several years. I made continuous changes and adjustments to my lists as I learned how to be more realistic about the time we have available and to make wise choices among all the options we have to choose from, and as I got better about figuring out what it was I really wanted to do.

If you never got into extensive list making, or were able to keep it under control, your job of simplifying may be easier than you thought.

22. Zero In on Your Top Four
or Five Priorities

There were many intermediate steps along the way, but I have only one list now. It looks something like this:

Spend time with Gibbs

Pursue my writing career

Have quiet time alone for my inner work

Spend time with family and friends

Have quiet time for reading and drawing

This is a far cry from my previous lists, but when I factor in all the activities of daily living—the things we have to do to survive, like food shopping, cooking, eating, sleeping—realistically, this is what I have time for.

It was a tremendous relief for me to look at all the other things I'd been carrying around on those lists, and to finally get the picture that there were simply not enough hours in the day or in the week or in the year to accomplish them all, and that I was going to have to let most of them go, at least for now.

In my experience, as people start to simplify their lives, the things that really matter naturally come to the forefront. Ideally, you reach the point where all the distractions have been minimized or eliminated from your life. The things that are important to you are so few and so obvious that you don't even need to write them down. Instead, by simplifying you've been able to arrange your life so that each day automatically revolves around those things.

If you're an incurable list maker, be open to the possibility that you may have to cut your lists back to more realistic proportions.

If you're not a list maker by nature or by habit, you might find it helpful to come up with a brief list of four or five things you'll want to concentrate on as you begin to simplify your life.

Just don't get carried away.

23. Remember, There Are Only Twenty-Four Hours in the Day

I have long been aware of the notion that there are only twenty-four hours in a day. But until I simplified, I hadn't stopped long enough to figure out how that frequently overlooked detail affected my life.

It's very deceptive. Twenty-four hours sounds like a lot of time, and so it feels as though we should be able to fit into the day all the things we think we have to do as well as all the things we want to do.

But the fact is if you work eight hours a day and sleep eight hours a night, that leaves only eight hours for everything else.

Most of us spend roughly half of those eight hours provisioning for, preparing, eating, and cleaning up after our meals; bathing, brushing, and flossing; finding the right necktie or looking for a pair of stockings without a run in them;

and if we're lucky, cycling, jogging, or walking around the block.

If you factor in commute time, housekeeping chores, mail sorting, bill paying, sex, social phone calls, duty phone calls, feeding the dog, cleaning out the cat's litter box, and scheduling the next day's activities, you can use up more than half of those four hours before you even turn on the TV or pick up a newspaper.

If you have child-related duties or volunteer commitments, or if you spend extra time at the office or excessive time commuting, that leaves approximately no quality time with your spouse, your kids, your friends, no quiet time alone, and no time for your creative interests, which are the things the majority of us agree are the most important.

We may believe, for example, that we can get ready to leave for the office in forty-five minutes. But the reality is that, in addition to all the things we have to do in that time to get dressed—shower, shave, blow dry, and stand in front of the closet for ten minutes trying to figure out what to wear—we also have to squeeze the orange juice, pack the kids' lunches, walk the dog, bring in the paper, and feed the cat. And we wonder why we're dashing out the door fifteen minutes late for the office.

We think we can do it all. But in the reality of the twenty-four-hour day, it seems unlikely. It takes a tremendous amount of time just to keep up with spouses who want our attention, kids who need our love, employers who demand our souls, homes that take a lot of our energy, friendships that require nurturing, and our own inner cravings that need to be met. That's enough for one twenty-four-hour day.

For many of us, all the other things we think we want to attend to will have to wait until they start making thirty-six-hour days.

24. Remember that Relationships Take Time

When you're zeroing in on what's important to you, keep in mind that our close relationships frequently need more time than we've devoted to them in recent years.

This seems so obvious, but given the fact that one out of three marriages ends in divorce and our children feel disenfranchised, it's apparently easy to overlook. Not that inattention is the only cause of divorce, but it's certainly a contributing factor.

Gibbs and I have always felt that our marriage was one of our very top priorities, but we'd gradually begun to devote more and more energy to our goals without realizing that the time we had for each other was getting lost in the shuffle.

Considering all the other pressures and the time demands that we allow to impinge on our day-to-day activities, it's easy to get into the habit of taking our closest relationships for granted.

I believe there's also a subtle tendency to think that once

we've landed the person of our dreams, we can check "get married" off our list. Then we move ahead, have our 2.3 children, and check "have children" off the list.

Then we get so caught up in the work we do to support these relationships—and the home, the cars, the clothes, and the never-ending cultural and social and educational activities that seem necessary—that we lose sight of the relationships themselves.

We can so easily end up with a variation of the famous Roy Lichtenstein cartoon of the 1980s. One that says, "Oh my God! I forgot to make time for my family."

If you're in a relationship or have children, these are no doubt going to be a top priority. Devote some of your newfound free time to your nearest and dearest.

25. Stop Feeding Your Ego

A few years ago I was asked to write book reviews for one of the major book clubs. At the time, I was delighted to accept this offer. It gave me the chance to keep up with the latest books in my field of investing, and it also gave me the opportunity to say that I was doing reviews for this prestigious book club.

While that sounded impressive, at least to my ear, the reality was that the work was intermittent, the manuscripts were often tedious, the deadlines were urgent, and the pay was lousy. As time went on, it became a major complication in my life.

As my field of interest changed, it would have been logical to discontinue this work. But I kept doing it far longer than I should have, somewhat out of habit, partly out of feeling fortunate to have been asked to do this thing (that I didn't really want to do), but mostly so I could continue to say, if only to myself, that I was doing reviews for this book club.

Eventually, I figured out that if I stopped doing the reviews, I could still say I *used* to do book reviews for this prestigious book club, and it would carry almost the same weight in terms of ego gratification. So I finally got wise, and retired from this activity.

Even though it's embarrassing for me to admit this, I know from talking to people that this kind of behavior is not un-usual.

We often get into work situations, social commitments, vol-unteer obligations, sports routines, and other types of activities that complicate our lives. We stay in them far longer than we need to because it looks good on paper, or because it sounds good when we have the opportunity to drop it into conversa-tions, or because in some way it meets our own or someone else's expectations of the kinds of things we think we should be doing.

We each have to decide for ourselves when it's appropriate to bow out of these kinds of endeavors. This might be a good time to take a look at your life and see if there are any activities you're involved in that are no longer serving a purpose for your simple life. Then drop them.

26. Learn to Make Good Choices

In order to simplify, we have to start making choices, sometimes difficult choices. And often it means saying no, even to the things we want to do.

Shortly after Gibbs and I began to take steps to simplify, we found ourselves having dinner with some friends who were into hang gliding.

We spent the entire evening listening to them rave about the thrill of this fascinating sport. As we sat there being seduced by yet another activity, we imagined ourselves leaping off the cliff and soaring silently over the beautiful hills behind our home.

By the time the evening was over we'd promised our friends we'd meet them at six o'clock the next morning on a nearby peak to try out their gear and have our first lesson.

All the way home we talked about how wonderful it would be to start hang gliding.

Then we walked through the front door, looked at each other, and reality began to set in. We reminded ourselves of how little time we actually have available. We realized there was no way we'd be able to fit a new sport into our schedule, especially one as time and energy consuming as hang gliding. We knew that our short list would suffer if we did. And our short list had been suffering long enough.

When we analyzed it carefully, we realized hang gliding was not as high on our list as we'd originally thought.

Reluctantly, we called our friends and explained why we wouldn't be able to join them.

"Sorry, we got carried away. We'd truly love to meet you tomorrow morning, but we're making some changes in our lives, and we simply won't have time to get involved in hang gliding for the time being."

When we thought about it later, we realized this was progress for us. In the past, we'd have purchased all the equipment and had six weeks of lessons before it dawned on us that we couldn't fit this new activity into our schedule.

And all the time, we'd have been wondering why, when we

were at last engaged in this wonderful activity that we both had thought we wanted, our lives had become even more complicated and stressed out. The choices then would have been to stop hang gliding and feel guilty about all the time and money we'd wasted, or to keep trying to justify the expenditure by continuing with an endeavor that we didn't have time for.

The need to make wise choices encompasses every area of our lives. Since we have time for only a limited amount of stuff, we need to choose wisely what stuff we're going to allow to take up that time. Since we have only a limited amount of time to spend with friends or to engage in leisure activities, we need to choose our friends and our activities wisely.

Take a look at your own life to see if there are any choices you might be able to make that would free up more time and energy for the things that are higher up on your list.

27. Set Your Time Management System Aside

If you've got an extensive list of all the things you want to do or feel you have to do, how do you get to a simple list?

One possibility is to try a fresh approach.

One of the best things I did when I went on my four-day retreat was to leave behind that time management system with the interminable lists.

No doubt there are people who wouldn't agree with this tactic. After all, frequently our whole lives—our goals, our aspirations, our life purpose, our priorities, our to-do lists—are laid out in those systems. And we've become addicted to them. We've spent untold dollars learning to use them, and countless hours keeping up with the process.

But many of us have found that those systems don't manage as well as we'd thought they would. I finally began to suspect that my lists were part of the problem.

In addition to including all the things we think we want to do, often our goal lists reflect what we feel we ought to do. In many cases these lists are determined, sometimes without our even recognizing it, by outside influences such as career demands, peer pressures, parental expectations, family obligations, or media enticements. Frequently we've lost touch with what we truly want to do.

I looked at one of the bestselling books on time management recently. The charts, lists, goal planners, and other strategies required to manage our hectic days made my head spin. It's my belief that those systems don't simplify our lives; often they assist us in keeping them complicated.

Even more insidious is the subtle underlying message in many of these systems that somehow we're missing out on life, or in some way are not doing our part if each day isn't scheduled down to the last minute.

I'm not suggesting that you shelve your time management system permanently, but merely that you set it aside as you figure out what matters.

It may well be that some of those things that matter are already on one of your existing lists. That's okay. The idea here is to let the list you'll be forming now come from your heart rather than from your own or someone else's expectations.

As you reduce the stress and time demands of your hectic life, your new list may turn out, as mine did, to be not only shorter, but quite different than you expected.

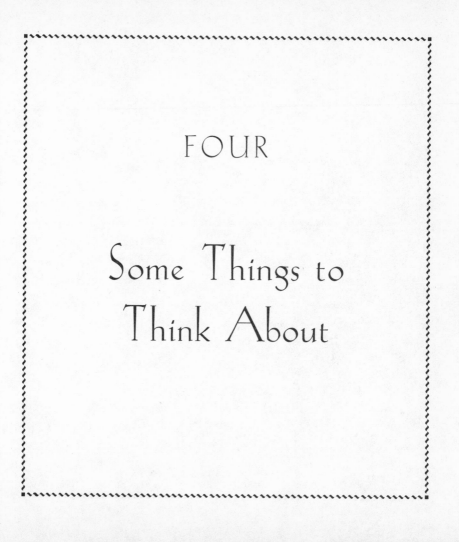

FOUR

Some Things to Think About

28. Simplifying Is Often Two Steps Forward, One Step Back

One of the things Gibbs and I did to simplify was to get rid of a lot of the clutter in our lives. That was two big steps forward for us.

It took us several weeks to complete this process and it was several more weeks before we could hold a garage sale to unload the stuff, so in the interim our living space was in a state of chaos. That was a temporary step back.

Then, after the thrift store truck pulled out of the driveway with everything we couldn't unload in the garage sale, we decided to move to a smaller house. Two steps forward.

We went through another month of disruption until we could get into our new place. One step back.

It was another week or so before we were completely settled into our small but cozy condo. Two steps forward.

It was only a couple of months later that we noticed we were going out and acquiring things to fill it up again. Ten steps back.

One of Gibbs's objectives in simplifying was to have time to devote to some of his volunteer projects, and so he started reading for Recording for the Blind. Two steps forward.

A year later he stopped one day and realized that in addition to his weekly reading, he was also now participating in the local adult literacy program and had become an active member of the Coast Guard Auxiliary. He was beginning to feel overwhelmed again. One step back.

When I made the decision to write *Inner Simplicity*, I realized I had found a new career possibility. A major step forward in terms of finding my life's work.

But I committed to a tight deadline, which meant I wrote practically around the clock during that time. Even though I loved what I was doing, it was definitely two steps back in terms of scheduling balance into my routine.

It might be helpful to know that the two step one step phenomenon can occur on the way to living the simple life. The habits of a fast-paced life die slowly. And change by its very nature is disruptive. Even with the best planning, it may not be possible to avoid periods of upheaval and disorder—and possibly even confusion—on the way to a simple life.

29. Be Aware of the Pitfalls of Having Extra Time on Your Hands

Making changes in your schedule so you can free up an hour or two every morning for the next month will make it possible for you to start making some dramatic changes in your life.

It can also be terrifying. Or tremendously challenging. You might feel guilty. Or you might want to run screaming back to some time-consuming drama so you don't have to deal with the real issues. Or it can be all of the above.

Keep in mind that the complications in our lives can take on a momentum of their own. They can rapidly expand to fill the time allotted for them. They can also expand to fill time that is not allotted for them. Stay focused, and no matter how strong the temptation, don't let the latest crisis—yours or anyone else's—eat into your newfound time.

This is one reason to schedule some of your quiet time away from your usual setting where most of the distractions occur with predictable regularity.

If you're in the habit of feeling rushed and overpowered by your schedule, don't allow that habit to carry over into your new free time. Make a concerted effort, especially in the early stages of simplifying, to stay loose and relaxed.

You may reach a point where it feels as though it would just be simpler to continue with your hectic life. It's clear to me now that one of the reasons I maintained a complicated life was because I was afraid of what I'd have to unravel in order to simplify it. Having taken major steps to eliminate the complexities of my life, I can assure you that, even in the short run, simplifying is easier once you've taken the plunge.

Also, remember we know how to move at breakneck speed, so at one level that feels comfortable. Most of us haven't had as much practice moving slowly, so doing so with ease can be a real challenge.

Be prepared for change. When I simplified, my whole life was transformed dramatically: I reduced my living space by more than half, I moved away from relationships that weren't working, I let go of a lot of my limiting beliefs, I found a new career, and was compelled, ultimately, to confront a lot of my inner demons. All this can make you feel like you're standing at the edge of a cliff.

If you find yourself feeling uncomfortable with a lot of extra time on your hands, try to figure out exactly what it is you're experiencing. Identifying your reactions is the first step toward moving beyond them.

Don't let an initial feeling of discomfort keep you from making the changes you want to make in your life. Realize that once you get into the process and actually begin taking steps to simplify, you'll leave those feelings behind pretty quickly.

30. Get Off Automatic Pilot

One of the things that made it possible for me to keep going at high speed until I simplified my life was an innate ability to race through my day on automatic pilot. I think this is true for a lot of us.

We're used to rolling out of bed in the morning, moving quickly through our ablutions, grabbing a bite to eat while we read the paper or watch the morning news, packing the kids off to school or day care, putting the finishing touches on a report for the boss, having a final swig of coffee, then flying out the door to start our workday, without reflecting on what we're doing.

We take the same route to work, so we don't have to think about it, and our minds easily fill with a million other things—worries, responsibilities, obligations—on the way to the office.

While some of our daily work procedures are less automatic than others, there's still a certain predictability about a lot of the

111

tasks we take on. Mostly we don't have to analyze it much. We just get through the day so we can hop in the car, and go back home, on automatic.

Then we fall immediately into our evening schedule, what ever that might be for us: exercise, on automatic; dinner, on automatic; cleanup, on automatic; meetings, on automatic; watching television, on automatic.

The weekends are frequently the same, though they usually allow for a little more latitude in terms of the routine. But most of us tend to do the same things over and over again, week in and week out.

Yes, we may vary the specifics somewhat. We may have social or cultural or recreational outings on a regular basis. But those can easily become automatic as well. We tend to go to the same places, see the same people, discuss the same issues.

There's a certain comfort in moving through our lives this way. The world sometimes seems unpredictable, and the grooves we establish give us a feeling of order and of being in control. That's fine as long as the things we're doing on automatic are the things we really want to be doing. Often they're not—or maybe they were once but aren't now—and we haven't stopped long enough to realize it.

And paradoxically, living on automatic complicates our lives. Living on automatic is often what makes it possible for us to do all the things we feel we have to do. We squeeze into our days new chores or commitments, adding another errand here, another lunch date there, without considering whether we really have the time to do them, let alone the desire. We just take a deep breath, put our nose back to the grindstone, and add one more item to our list of things to do.

This is where building some air into our schedule pays off. We can create the time to have a leisurely breakfast with our family, or take the scenic route to the office and enjoy the ride. We can create daily and weekly variations that will make it possible for us to savor special moments throughout our days, throughout our weeks, and throughout our lives.

Changing gears from time to time makes it possible for us to get into the habit of being aware and alive each moment, or at least for a lot more of our moments. And the more aware we are, the easier it is to get back in control of our lives.

The process then builds on itself. Each time we become conscious of the fact that we're doing something we'd rather not be doing, we can make adjustments in our schedule. Gradually we can learn to eliminate those activities and substitute more appealing pursuits.

31. Some Ways to Change Gears

Here are some things you might think about doing to get off automatic for a bit:

Get up earlier and go out to eat with the family at a local breakfast dive. Or pack some muffins, juice, and coffee for a picnic breakfast to watch the sunrise.

Walk to work. Cycle to work. Take a bus to work. Take a different route to work.

Walk the kids to school instead of driving them.

Do your grocery shopping early in the morning before the store gets crowded. Shop at a different store altogether to get a fresh perspective on the items you purchase.

Meet your spouse and/or kids for lunch in the park. Or leave the office early, pick up a deli basket, and have dinner in the park at sunset.

Let the housekeeping go this week. Spend the time with your kids instead.

Let the laundry go this week. Or assign the routine chores to someone else if you can.

You might come up with a slightly different way of approaching these tasks that would make them simpler for the time being. Recently a friend of mine asked her 10-year-old to make her bed before guests arrived. "Can't we just close the bedroom door?" her daughter asked.

There are many circumstances in which just closing the door for the moment would make life simpler.

Take a vacation day in the middle of the week with your spouse and kids, and go play together. If you can't take the whole day, take the afternoon off together.

Exercise at a different time; or do it at a different place; or do it with someone else; or do it alone.

Unplug your phone for a week. Or change your outgoing message to say you'll return all calls next week. When I started simplifying some of my office protocol, I was amazed to learn how few phone calls need immediate attention.

Or sit in a different chair or at a different desk. If possible, work in a different office, or take your work to an empty table in the local library or your favorite café.

Take some time right now to come up with two or three things you could do this week that would help you break, even for a short while, the patterns that keep you moving through life on automatic, the patterns that keep you trying to do it all.

32. Involve Your Children in the Process of Simplifying

If you've got kids, your simplification program will obviously be easier to put into place if you include them in the process and enlist their help in making your lives simpler.

I hear wonderful stories from families who've worked together to simplify their lives. I also hear from teenagers who long for simplicity in their world. They've seen how all the complications, commitments, and stress have kept their parents from being happy, and they're determined not to let their lives be that hectic now, or get that overwhelming as they grow older.

It might be helpful to schedule a family powwow with the stated intention of setting up a program to simplify all your lives. You could start with a discussion designed to help everyone figure out what their own priorities are as well as what the family priorities are. Then take a close look at your schedules to see what kinds of changes you can make to free up time together as a family.

Assign each child chores in the preparation and cleanup of daily meals, and with the laundry, housekeeping, and yard maintenance. This will give the kids a feeling of responsibility for the family well-being and relieve some of the time pressures of the primary caretaker.

Not every family member is going to respond favorably to a plan to simplify. The ages of the children and the dynamics within the family will determine, to some extent, how receptive your kids may be to the idea of making some changes and simplifying. But don't automatically assume that your children will not be interested. With the pressures on kids today, they may be as ready to simplify as you are.

33. When Your Significant Other Doesn't Want to Simplify

It's one thing to get your children involved in your plans for simplifying or, if they're not interested, to work around them. But it can be another issue entirely if your spouse is not open to the idea.

If this is your predicament, don't give up on the idea of simplifying. There are a number of things you can do.

First, you can look at all the areas of your own life that you can simplify, such as your work life, your social life, your volunteer projects, your exercise routine, your wardrobe, your car, your desk, your side of the medicine cabinet, and so forth.

It's entirely possible that as you begin to simplify your life so you can do the things you really enjoy doing, your partner may be inspired and decide to join you. If nothing else, at least you'll have created energy to put up with someone who wants a complicated life.

Whatever you do, don't spend a whole lot of time trying to change the other person. If he or she is not interested in simplifying, the chances are good that no amount of nagging is going to transform them, and it will only complicate your life.

Another thing you can do is change your expectations about how simple their life has to be. It's possible that two people with disparate lifestyles can each make a valuable contribution to the other's life. If you love one another, and are close in many other areas, you may each have to allow the other to pursue his or her own level of complexity.

If, as often happens, the main issue is the other person's clutter, the situation can be tricky. Many people have a lot of stuff because they've never learned how to throw things out, but under the right circumstances, they would be open to learning.

Also, some people thrive on clutter and complexity, or think they do. It's possible they've never stopped to think about how clutter can get in the way of living their lives, or how it's getting in the way of your life. Often, these situations offer the potential for change, or at the very least, compromise.

But when you're dealing with someone whose clutter is a substitute for the love they never got as a child—or is a refuge from earlier abuse or deprivation—then you both might need to find professional help to deal with this issue.

If the situation is or becomes untenable for you, it may be necessary to consider a permanent change. Although this is obviously a drastic measure, I've heard from many people who've said that one of the most important steps they took was to move on from a spouse whose life was incompatible with their own desire to live simply.

Of course the other thing that can happen when one person starts devoting more time to the relationship is that the other person's priorities change. They, too, become more attentive, and so the whole relationship improves.

The other option is to try to find a friend (#34) who supports you in your desire to create a simple life and accept that, possibly for the time being, your spouse won't be joining you.

34. Find a Buddy

If you feel you need help creating a simpler life, and your partner is not enrolled for the moment in your simplicity program, then find a sympathetic friend, or two or three, and connect with them on a regular basis so you can share ideas and provide encouragement as needed.

Having even one other person who understands and approves of your need to simplify will make your task a lot easier. Our desire to simplify our lives goes against the mainstream in this culture, so going it alone can be a real challenge.

If you have just one person supporting you in this, plan to connect by phone at least once or twice a week. Limit your phone calls to ten to fifteen minutes, or less if possible. It's so easy to launch into a lengthy discussion that can derail your intention to have time for yourself.

If there are three or four of you committed to simplifying, it might make more sense to arrange for a weekly meeting where you can all get together and share in round-robin fashion.

For five people, for example, you could plan to meet for an hour and a half, allowing fifteen minutes for each person to share their own experiences from the week, followed by a wrap-up for fifteen minutes or so.

Agree on the meeting arrangement in advance so you can launch right in without wasted time or effort. Use the wrap-up to evaluate the effectiveness of your session and determine whether or not you need to make any changes in the process.

Make this gathering a model of simplification. Eliminate the extraneous stuff, such as refreshments, that quickly become one more complication in your life. For now, the goal is to use the group meeting as an aid to get to the simple life as efficiently as possible.

35. How to Deal with People Who Don't Understand

In making the decision to simplify your life, you run the risk of going against the generally accepted American standard of success. Friends and associates who are still looking to Madison Avenue or to corporate America or the media to define what success is for them may well find your desire for a simpler life tantamount to heresy. They'll think you've gone soft. Or that maybe you just don't have what it takes to succeed in the "real" world.

Sometimes—though they wouldn't admit it—they see your new lifestyle as a threat to their own.

To many, the idea of paring down and living a simple life seems not only impractical, it's unthinkable. The question often is, "Why would you want to have only a little when you can have a lot? Or even have it all?"

The reactions you receive can range anywhere from friendly teasing, to well-intentioned advice about hanging in there, to outright ostracism.

And you may go through your own period of confusion. If you've spent a good deal of your life in recent years allowing your professional persona to define who you are, not only to yourself, but to your family, your friends, your colleagues, and your community, you may sometimes find yourself in situations where it's a real challenge to let go of that identity.

As you move along in your plan to simplify, take whatever time you feel is necessary to explain to friends your plan to create a life outside the narrow confines of what passes for success in the world. But don't be surprised if they don't immediately join you in your quest.

It takes courage to buck the tide, but once you start to experience the freedom that comes from actively creating your own interpretation of success, you'll find it easy to move on from people who haven't yet figured out that having it all or spending long hours at an unsatisfying job will never define who they truly are, no matter how high the pay.

You'll no doubt soon reach the point, where you can say, as Cynthia Ferguson did (#3), "I've stopped trying to explain to people. Now I just let them wonder why I seem so happy and secure in myself these days."

36. Find a Happy Medium That Works for You

One of the things I did in the early stages of our simplification program was to get rid of our houseplants. Our cat, Speed—named after a strong female character from one of Gibbs's novels—was a strong female cat who got into the habit of eating the leaves of the plants; then she'd throw up on the carpet. It got to be such a hassle that it came down to deciding whether to get rid of the plants or to get rid of the cat.

Because Speed is such a wonderful cat in every other respect, we decided the houseplants would have to go.

It was only after I'd passed my plants on to friends and neighbors that I saw how much effort they'd been. As one reader wrote, "I had never realized how time consuming my houseplants were. They're like kids—you've got to feed them, water them, and pick up after them. Like you, I got rid of all my plants and simplified my life!"

But after several years without plants, I reached a point where I missed having them. I also realized that one of the reasons they'd been such a complication earlier was that my plant population had gotten out of control—I'd had far too many of them.

A while back a friend gave me a beautiful Phalenopsis orchid and I've found, to my delight, that this is one plant Speed won't touch. Orchids are low-maintenance plants that require minimal care, never drop their leaves, and have an exquisite bloom that lasts for months. So now I have a couple of gorgeous orchids around the house that I enjoy immensely. Not only are they beautiful, but they're so simple.

So, in getting rid of *all* the plants, I'd gotten carried away. Even though it simplified my life in the beginning stages to be free of them, I eventually found that having one or two beautiful plants added a lot to my life. I'd come back to a happy medium for me.

Just be aware that you may have to take some drastic steps in the early stages of simplifying your life that will make things easier for you during the process of getting to simple—such as cutting out the newspapers, eliminating some of the routine household chores, or temporarily dropping a lot of your social activities.

Then, as you achieve a certain level of comfort and ease by simplifying other areas of your life, you may decide to go back to some of your previous practices. Or you may find that by doing them differently from the way you did when your life was hectic, they can contribute something to your life in their new incarnation.

37. Keep Asking, "Is This Going to Simplify My Life?"

As Gibbs and I went through the process of simplifying, we got into the habit of asking ourselves, "Is this going to simplify our lives?" every time we considered a potential purchase, or a new service, or a change to our routine.

For example, one of the things we thought we wanted to do, as we were offloading many of the possessions we'd accumulated during our hard-charging years, was cut back to one car. Since I work at home and Gibbs now had an easy ten-minute commute to his office, we thought that with a bit of judicious planning, we could easily get by with only one set of wheels.

So when we moved to the condo and found ourselves on a bus line that provided direct access to Gibbs's place of work, we thought, Aha! Now is the time to get rid of the old Plymouth.

But before we did, we decided to try the bus schedule. It worked well for some months, until Gibbs's office setup changed and the bus schedule was no longer convenient. And at the same time, my schedule required that I spend more time on the road and so I needed the car more than I had.

We were still philosophically disposed to getting rid of one of the cars, but the reality was that, given our new schedule and the limited public transportation in a part of the country that relies heavily on the automobile, it wouldn't actually simplify our lives to do so.

At another point we were doing some minor renovations to our home and had drawn up a list of the changes we wanted to make. By this time we'd gotten into the habit of asking ourselves, "Is this going to simplify our lives?" So we went down the list and were able to eliminate over half the things we'd originally thought we'd need to have done.

Yes, it would simplify our lives to replace the aging, small-capacity washer that tended to mangle the clothes and the decrepit dryer that had only one setting (fry). And, yes, adding a kitty door to the cat box would simplify not only the cleanup and maintenance, but would provide more space in the already limited closet where the cat box was housed.

But the kitchen countertops were fine, and replacing them would add nothing to their serviceability, but a good deal to the expense and a lot of disruption to our lives in the interim. It was simpler to leave them as they were.

Our culture is replete with so-called convenience items—call waiting, E-mail, the food processor—or alternative approaches to situations that at first glance appear to be simplifiers, or which might simplify someone else's life, but which on closer inspection would only complicate our own.

We've found the habit of asking "Will this really simplify our lives?" a powerful weapon in the ongoing battle against the complications of modern life.

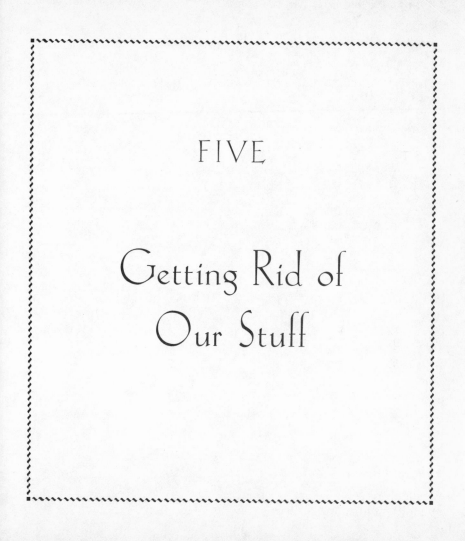

FIVE

Getting Rid of
Our Stuff

38. Where to Start

If you're ready to begin unloading the stuff that's been cluttering up your life, and you don't know where to start, start with the easy stuff.

I heard from a woman recently who had an office full of files, family papers, legal documents, reports, journal articles and other paraphernalia for projects she had worked on.

She knew she needed to bite the bullet, go through all that stuff, make some difficult decisions about what to keep, and eventually throw out a lot of it. But because it seemed like such a monumental task, she couldn't seem to get going on it.

So I suggested she leave the office alone for the time being, and start somewhere else. Like with the linens.

Has there ever been a linen closet that wasn't chock full of well-worn, mismatched sheets that will never be used again? Or sheets that may be in perfectly good shape, but that fit the bed you gave away three years ago? Or stacks of bath towels and washcloths that don't match your current color scheme and you'll never again hang on a towel rack?

What about the tablecloths and napkin sets that you haven't used in years because you can't bear the thought of ironing them? You know you'll never use that stuff again. Pass it on to someone who can.

The kitchen is often another safe place. Start with the very top shelves in the kitchen cabinets. Get rid of anything that is covered with a thin coating of grime—it's a safe bet you haven't used it in a while, and probably never will again.

Pull out all the so-called convenience items such as the bread makers, plate warmers, and the pasta machines you've only used once in five years, and pass them along to someone who might like to have them. (They won't use those things more than once or twice either, but at least they won't be sitting on your shelves collecting dust.)

Look at any other areas in your home where it would be easy for you to go in and clear out—under the sinks, or the shelves in the laundry room, or the inner depths of the basement, perhaps the front hall closet, and start tossing.

This sounds so obvious, but often people feel trapped by the things they're afraid to let go of or that they know will be difficult for them to deal with, so they never get started at all. But if you get going with the easy stuff, and you see how good it feels to be free of it, it's so much easier to go on to the harder stuff.

Once you're in the decluttering mode, get to the hard stuff as quickly as you can. One of the objectives here is to use the momentum you've generated on the easy things to propel you into the discarding mode for the harder stuff.

As reader Nancy Hawkins wrote, "After buying and trying to follow books about how to be organized I was thrilled to realize I needed to simplify and *get rid of the clutter*, not just rearrange piles of stuff in a new way."

It's so true. If you just get rid of the clutter you never have to *organize* it.

39. Getting Rid of the Stuff Doesn't Necessarily Mean Getting Rid of *Everything*

Invariably when I talk to groups about simplifying and the issue of clutter comes up, someone will say something like, "I've gone through and cleared out a lot of stuff in my home, but I've got this stash of medals from when I was an Olympic swimmer. I know they're taking up space and I never wear them or even look at them much anymore, but I can't bear to throw them out. What do you suggest?"

Sometimes, it's a box of mementos, or a record collection, or their grandmother's fine china. My answer is simple. If you can't bear to throw them out, then *don't*.

Gibbs and I both love books. We love reading them. We love having them in our home. When we first started clearing out stuff, we had no intention of thinning out our collection of books. They meant too much to us.

Then, after we'd gotten rid of a driveway full of stuff we

weren't using anymore, and we experienced the tremendous feeling of liberation that comes from unloading, we decided to rethink our position on the books.

We went through the shelves and started pulling down tomes we knew we'd never read again. Some we sold to a local used-book shop. Others we donated to our public library. Every year or so we have gone through and pulled out more books that we now see we can do without.

But we still have a lot of books, and I can't imagine we'll ever get rid of every one of them. After all, one of the main reasons we simplified our lives was so we'd have time to do the reading we want to do.

Getting rid of the clutter is not about letting go of things that are meaningful to you. It's about letting go of the things that no longer contribute to your life so you have the time and the energy and the space for the things that do.

Also, keep in mind that our identities are often connected to our stuff. When we start unloading it, it feels like we're giving away part of ourselves. But unloading some of it can also help us move into the self we want to be.

40. Look at All the Things You Hold on to Because You Might Need Them Someday

As we were getting ready for the garage sale that would clear out of our lives forever all the things we had decided to let go on round one of our uncluttering process, we stopped for a brief moment and looked at all the stuff we had piled in the driveway.

Gibbs pointed out that we'd been holding on to most of this stuff on the theory that we *might need it someday.*

It's so easy to do this. You come across some seemingly fabulous thing you have no earthly use for at the moment, but you think, "I never know when I might need a whatever-this-is." And you put it on the back shelf somewhere (along with all the other things you never know when you might need).

And you think, "Well, it doesn't take much room, and it's not hurting anything. I'll keep it on hand just in case I ever need it."

But often these are things you have to keep clean, or maybe you have to wrap them carefully so they don't get broken. Sometimes these things are so valuable you have to insure them. If nothing else, you have to provide that back shelf for them. And so, at some level, they are weighing on your consciousness and impinging on your life.

As we stood in the driveway that day we realized that if there was something we ever did need from all this stuff, we could, in a pinch, go out and get it again. In fact, we could've replaced the entire driveway full of stuff for a few hundred dollars.

But the interesting thing is that now, five years later, there hasn't been even one thing we wished we'd held on to.

Well, there *was* an old pair of cowboy boots I put in the pile because they'd been sitting in the closet, unused, for some time. I was afraid they were housing a black widow spider and didn't want to put my hand in there to find out. Later, I kind of wished I'd saved them. But when I remember them accurately I know that they were so worn-out I never would have worn them again.

But other than that, nothing.

So, if you ever find yourself tempted to put something on the back shelf because you think you might need it someday, remember that *replacing* it (and all the other things on the back shelf you think you might need) is probably a lot easier than maintaining the space required to store it all.

And if you ever find yourself wistfully wishing you'd held on to something, it's seldom as wonderful or as suitable for your needs as you remember it being.

41. One Knife, One Fork, One Spoon

Reader Grace Samis described what I've found to be a great simplifier for many areas of the house where stuff tends to accumulate.

She wrote, "I'm working on having only two items more of 'things' than people that live in the house…meaning plates, glasses, cups, knives, forks, spoons, pillows, blankets, sheets, towels, etc. For example, if there are four people in the household, keep only six plates.

"This is a threefold treasure. First, this gives you more space in your household. Second, it forces you to keep up with the cleaning—you can't let the dishes pile up if you need them for the next meal. Third, and most importantly, you can't have unwanted guests over too often. With no extra plates, no extra pillows, no extra blankets, uninvited visitors can't just come for a casual visit for any great length of time without some hard planning!"

I love this idea for a number of reasons. First, it gives you a specific goal to work toward in the ongoing process of uncluttering. Once you set this limit—or any other limit that works for you—there's no guessing. No wondering, should I keep this or that. It's so easy: Just two more things than people, and everything beyond that goes out or to someone else who can use it.

Secondly, it not only frees up more space in the household—in the kitchen cabinets, bath cabinets, linen closet—it makes it so much easier to keep track of things. I know I've got exactly what I need for our own use, and then just two more. No more digging around in the back of closets or pulling out the stepladder to climb to the top shelf of the pantry, because I think there might be something useful back there. Now I know what's there, and it's only two more than what I use everyday.

Obviously, if you entertain a lot, this wouldn't work—unless you were open to the idea of keeping some disposable plates and utensils on hand. Or, you could go for a variation on the potluck meal and have people bring their own knives and forks and spoons.

Of course, Grace, the ultimate way to deal with unwanted houseguests is to learn to just say no(#57). But this is a workable solution until we can learn to do that.

42. Start Over Again, and Do It Right

I've heard from and talked to many people who described how Mother Nature simplified their lives for them. They'd lost their home and many or all of their possessions through fires, floods, earthquakes, mudslides, or some other disaster. Losing everything you own under such circumstances can be devastating, but the people I've heard from all saw their loss, ultimately, as a blessing.

"The fire saved us the agony of deciding what to keep and what to get rid of," one woman wrote. And once all those things were no longer there, she and her husband saw how they had weighed them down and complicated their lives.

"There was so much stuff we never used and that was just taking up space. We vowed when we started over, we'd replace only what we needed, and this time we'd do it right. We've kept our promise: We don't have much now, but what we have is exactly what we want."

Though we've never had a catastrophic loss such as that, Gibbs and I did have a close call shortly before we decided to simplify. At that time we lived in a fire zone. One night a firestorm raged through and destroyed over six hundred homes in our community. That tragedy gave us the opportunity to look objectively at the goods we'd accumulated.

We saw that there was so much we could get rid of and not only never miss, but be better off without. Having almost lost it all, we found it much easier to let go of the things we knew we'd never use again.

Obviously, there's a tremendous difference between geting rid of possessions and losing them through a natural disaster without having a say in the matter. And this is not to minimize the tragedy and pain such a loss can generate.

But you might think about how you would approach the acquisition process if you had it to do all over again. Look around your home and make a list of what you would replace.

Make another list of things you wouldn't acquire again no matter what, and in fact would be happy to be rid of.

When you're ready to start unloading some of your stuff, that list will be a good place to start.

43. Take a Picture of It

The young woman with the collection of medals and awards from her Olympic swimming days was in a quandary. She had just moved to a smaller, simpler place and wanted to keep a sparse, clean look to her life for the moment. She couldn't bear to get rid of the medals altogether, yet she didn't want them cluttering up her space.

She brought this up at a talk I gave, and one of the other members of the audience suggested that she sort the items, set aside the ones that had the most meaning for her, lay them out in an interesting arrangement, and take a photograph of them. Or she might photograph them individually, and create a photo montage she could hang on the wall.

Or she could simply photograph them, donate them to a school or an art class where they could be used by students for various projects, and keep the photos in a file folder.

This last idea appealed to her. She had already made the decision to keep the walls of her new space free of distractions, at least for the time being.

A photo montage wouldn't work for everything, but you might consider it as a possibility.

Don't let the photos clutter up your life, however. Many people wrote to say that photos, perhaps more than any other personal item, can clutter up closets, drawers, desks, shelves, and multiple nooks and crannies. If this is true in your house, gather from all the corners of your home every photograph you've taken or that has been given to you over your lifetime. Sort through them, mercilessly tossing out any shot that's out of focus, or that is of someone you've never seen before, or that you never want to be reminded of again. Arrange the remaining photos in albums in whatever order seems appropriate. This will eliminate a lot of clutter and provide a simple and enjoyable way for you to share family memories.

44. Never Touch a Piece of Mail More than Once

I'd heard about this approach to the seemingly endless torrent of paper that flows across our desks and through our lives. And for years I'd thought, "It might work for others, but it would never work for me." I felt I always had too much stuff coming in at any one time to handle it all right then and there. So I'd set it aside, and then I'd have to come up with *a lot more time* to handle *a lot more of it* later.

When I simplified my life, I did cut back on the number of journals, magazines, and newspapers that come into my home and office every day. I also drastically reduced the junk mail I was subjected to (#45).

As I began to simplify even more, and started letting go of a lot of the real estate and other business associations that generated a heavy load of mail, not only were there far fewer bills coming in each day, but eventually I arranged for the bills that did show up to be handled by automatic payment through my bank (#80).

But after hearing over and over again from readers of Simplify Your Life that handling it once was a major simplifier, I decided to try it.

Now I set aside an hour at the end of my workday to read the mail and to deal with the stream of paper that comes through the door. Most days it takes only a few moments to sort through the mail, send off a postcard response as needed, read any pertinent articles or newsletters, file anything I might need to refer to later, and toss out what I don't need to keep.

The better I get at making decisions on the spot as to what to keep, the more I can toss into the recycling bin, and the less stuff I have to file.

I also found it doesn't work to think "I can't read this article now, or make that decision at this moment," and set it aside for later. When I do that, I'm soon right back where I started, inundated with paperwork. But by keeping that hour at the end of the day to read it now, or to do whatever I need to do to make a decision now—place a phone call or do some research—I can usually deal with it immediately and be finished with it. We have to decide at some point what to do with it. I've learned it's better to decide now.

It's so liberating not to have stacks of paper weighing down the edges of my desk and the corners of my mind. Now the mail is all taken care of in just a few minutes or at the most an hour each day.

If it takes more than the allotted hour to deal with a particular item, then I'll set it aside for the next afternoon. Though now that I've gradually reduced the volume of mail and have increased my ability to decide right now how to deal with something, I seldom have to deal with it later.

If it takes less than the allotted hour to deal with the day's mail, which now it usually does, then I've got a sweet little bit of leisure time which I can use to stroll through the garden, call a friend, or just sit quietly and do nothing.

Learning to handle it only once ranks high on the list of steps I've taken to keep the clutter to a minimum.

This also applies to magazines and newspapers. I heard from

many people who simplified their lives by reading the morning paper as soon as it arrives, then passing it on to a friend or neighbor or taking it into the office to share with a co-worker. Not only does this practice reduce the clutter that otherwise often stays in your life, but it reduces the expense of newspaper and magazine subscriptions. As with many aspects of simplifying, it has some positive effects on the environment as well. If everyone did it we could drastically reduce the amount of paper that has to be produced for these products and, ultimately, cut back on the volume of paper that has to be recycled each day.

45. Junk Mail Update

Junk mail is certainly one of the major complications of modern life, and few things add more useless stuff to our clutter. In *Simplify Your Life* I describe how we cut back on the amount of junk mail that comes into our home by writing to the Mail Preference Service (P.O. Box 9008, Farmingdale, NY, 22735-9008) and requesting that our name not be sold to any mailing list companies.

As my friend Donna wrote from Chicago, that's a start, but there is much more you can do. She says, "I cut my mail down from literally two cubic feet a week to just a neat handful a day by applying the techniques in the booklet *Stop Junk Mail Forever* by Marc Eisenson (available from Good Advice Press, Elizaville, NY, 12523 (914) 758-1400 for $4.50). The notification of mail preferenced service alone won't do it. I found out my professional journals, professional organizations, auto insurance, charge cards, credit bureaus, and so on, were all selling my name. Also, standardizing my name and address on our self-inking stamper helped so I wouldn't get on different lists due to variant spellings, for example, without middle initial, spelling out North instead of abbreviating. I've got a little stamp made up in a red ink: DO NOT LEASE SELL TRADE MY NAME ADDRESS. My mail carrier is very appreciative too."

I took Donna's advice and ordered this booklet. In my opinion, it's worth its weight in gold. In addition to information on how to contact the Mail Preference Service, it lists roughly eighteen steps you can take to literally stop junk mail forever, and to stop unwanted phone calls, too.

It took me less than an hour to call (when 800 numbers were available) or to send a postcard to the junk mail handling organizations listed in this booklet, requesting that our names be removed from all the major lists. It has made an incredible difference in the amount of mail I have to deal with each day. And it has also greatly reduced the number of temptations we're exposed to in the form of glossy four-color catalogs filled with stuff no one really needs.

If you're burdened by junk mail or telephone solicitations, order this book.

46. Don't Even Think about Saving That Piece of Aluminum Foil

We've all heard the stories about the little old lady who passed on, leaving her heirs a ball of string the size of a Buick or a mountain-high stack of newspapers she'd never had time to read. Or the drawers full of stubby and broken pencils and now stretchless rubber bands that no one would ever use, even if they were the last rubber bands on the planet.

Maybe you have an accumulation of these, or similarly useless items, sequestered away somewhere. If you do, you may be ahead of the game: With an ample supply of such superfluous material, you'll never have to save another piece of string or a thumbtack with a bend on the pointy end.

I never had a problem with coupons whose expiration date had passed or last year's denomination of stamps—at least not a *serious* problem. But for years my downfall was used 8 1/2 x 11-inch envelopes.

Being married to a writer/editor who is constantly receiving manuscripts in large manila envelopes, I had a prodigious and never-ending supply of used envelopes. As a new manuscript came in, I could never throw out that envelope. I clung to it tenaciously on the theory that I might need it someday. One or two, possibly. But hundreds?

When I started clearing out the clutter, I took a huge gulp and eliminated all but a dozen used manilas. I've trained myself, with some effort, so that I put them in the recycling bin instead of bringing them into my office. Whenever the mail carrier delivers another one, I repeat to myself, slowly and with great feeling, *don't even think about saving this envelope.*

I've been able to let go of most of the inessentials. By using this mantra I now have merely a dozen used manila envelopes I'll never use, rather than hundreds of them. Well, nobody's perfect.

You might find it helpful to come up with a similar mantra for the times you're tempted to squirrel away any of the items you tend to stockpile. Things like used plastic wrap, newspaper clippings you'll never look at again, magazines with an article you'd like to read if you could only remember what relevance it had to your life, extensions of pipe that won't work for any plumbing repair job you'll ever attempt in this lifetime, milk cartons you'll never use to make candles, bits of fabric you'll never turn into quilts, twisties past their prime, the small pad of address labels sent by a worthy charity printed with your former address, the small boxes of business cards from a company you haven't worked for in five years, a 1992 telephone directory, ballpoint pens that no longer have ink, sprung paper clips, keys whose provenance is unknown, bald emery boards, broken sunglasses, ID tags for the previous dog, bus tokens for the Topeka Transit System when you live in Duluth and have no plans to return to Kansas, and the plastic doohickey that used to fit something though you haven't a clue what. You won't remember what it used to fit until you throw it out. If you ever could retrieve it, you'd find that it didn't fit what you thought it did anyway.

Next time you find yourself standing in front of the drawer into which you're planning to tuck away a bit of thrice-used foil too small to keep, let yourself go, and throw it out.

47. Use Your Public Library

I've used the library extensively for years, but it wasn't until I started getting letters from readers, especially from mothers with young children, that I began to recognize the extent to which it could minimize the clutter.

Public libraries are for most people an easy and readily available solution for cutting back on the amount of stuff that comes into our homes, not only in terms of the books we read, but also in terms of magazines, newspapers, newsletters, audiotapes, videotapes, CDs, reference sources, and information services of almost limitless variety.

In addition to providing an ever-ready source of the latest books and reading material at minimal or no cost, public libraries also, through the ever-impending due date, supply the impetus to read these materials in a timely fashion. While we may not read every single book or magazine we bring home from the library, at least they won't be cluttering up our night-stands and bookshelves on a permanent basis; at some point we have to take them back to the library.

Libraries also supply a practical way to offload the stacks of your own books and audio- and videotapes that are cluttering up your environment. Not only will donating books to the library free up space in your home and office, but it provides such a simple and satisfying way to share your resources with others.

At the very least, when you donate books to the library—if your library keeps them—you always know where they are should you want to read them again. You can thereby have your books and not have them at the same time. It's hard to get simpler than that.

48. Get Some Help

I hear from people all the time who, once they saw how much it would simplify their lives to get rid of the clutter, jumped right in and started throwing stuff out. But many are not inclined to move so quickly and could use some hand-holding through this process. If you need some help, get it.

Ask a family member, one of your simplicity buddies, or a friend who knows you well to help you. You want someone who has the strength of character to overlook your whines and half-hearted entreaties when you want to hold on to thirty years of *National Geographic* magazines and throws them out anyway, but who has the heart to let you keep your high school yearbooks.

Pick your starting point—the attic, the closets, or wherever. If you really want to be brave, take a deep breath, and have them go through the attic *without* you: Let them make the decisions about what to get rid of. You don't have a clue what's in those boxes anyway. So how can you possibly miss them?

Or establish some parameters ahead of time. They can throw out anything that was made prior to 1990. They can get rid of any clothes, but they can't touch the books.

I did this with a friend who couldn't bear to get rid of a lot of the clothes in her closet, even though she knew there were many things she'd never wear again. I went through the closet with her standing by, but we decided that I would make the initial decision regarding what stayed and what went out. (It's so much easier to toss it on the out pile when it's not yours.) When we were finished, she could go back through the stack and retrieve three items.

Then we made arrangements for a local thrift store to haul the rest away quickly, before she could change her mind. It was such a relief for her not to have to make the decisions about what had to go.

Not only does this relieve you of the responsibility of deciding what to get rid of, but you can always blame *them* if you decide later that there was something you would have kept!

If you don't trust your friends or family in this sometimes delicate task, another alternative is to hire a personal organizer to help you. If you can't locate one in the yellow pages, contact the National Association of Professional Organizers at 1033 La Posada Drive, Suite 220, Austin, Texas 78752 to see if they can refer you to a professional organizer in your area.

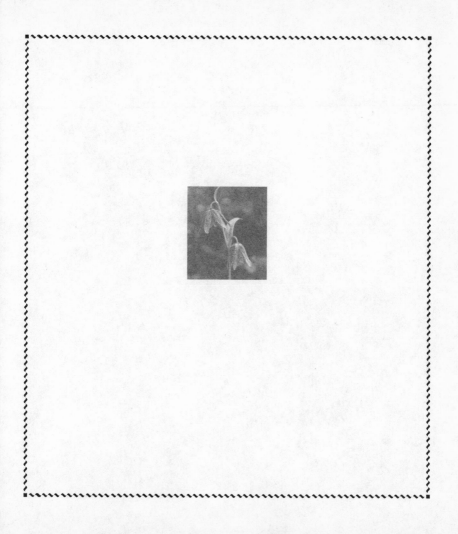

SIX

Changing Our Consumer Habits

49. The Thirty-Day List

Now that we've addressed ways to get rid of some of your stuff, let's talk about what you can do to keep the clutter from piling up again.

Have you ever found yourself wandering through a department store and coming across something you felt you just had to have? It's entirely possible that until you saw it on display, you didn't even know it existed. But now that you've seen it, you want it. And you want it now.

Often, whether you need it or not, whether you can afford it or not, whether you truly want it or not, you buy it, and bring it home. Maybe you use it once or twice, or even half a dozen times.

Eventually you come across this thing lying around the house somewhere and you wonder why on earth you ever bought it to begin with. Invariably, it ends up on that back shelf.

This scenario is played out over and over again in the lives of millions of people every day. Why? Because advertisers spend billions of dollars each year training us to react this way. It's a safe bet for their money—experience has shown we can be convinced to buy *anything*.

After Gibbs and I got rid of a lot of clutter and moved to our smaller place, we noticed, as I mentioned earlier, that we were going out and buying stuff to fill it up again. We realized we were going to have to change our buying patterns.

We decided to set up a thirty-day list. If we came across a significant item we thought we wanted, we'd put it on this list before we'd rush out to buy it. If at the end of thirty days we could remember what it was for, we might consider acquiring it. Or, we had the option at that point to extend the date for another thirty days. More often than not, at the end of the first thirty days, we couldn't remember why we wanted this thing in the first place.

You might consider using a similar system to keep youself and other family members from rushing to buy the next thing you see advertised that you think you want. It does require a modicum of discipline, but not only will it save you a considerable bundle of money, it will greatly reduce the amount of stuff which comes into your home that you then eventually have to get rid of.

50. Watch for the Early Warning Signs

Another thing we found helpful in the process of changing our buying habits was to become aware of the early warning signs of a potential buying transaction. There were at least two major signals we could learn to recognize and do something about.

First there are the physiological signs. You may find yourself innocently browsing when you quite unexpectedly come across something you think you'd like to buy. You'll begin to feel a slight palpitation of the heart. Soon your pulse starts to quicken. You feel a rush of adrenaline. Part of you wants to hold back. Another part of you is reaching for your credit card. You may experience shortness of breath. You might even salivate. In extreme cases you start to drool, though not so much that anyone would notice.

Then come the psychological rationalizations. You hear yourself listing all the reasons you should have this thing. You need it.

It'll make your life better. You deserve it. You've earned it, for godsake. It's on sale! It's been ages since you splurged a little. We only live once. It's only a hundred bucks. Your whole psyche is itching for this thing.

The itch is a critical juncture. Once you start to scratch it, it's all over.

This is where you train yourself to pull out your thirty-day list—the list on which you write down every significant item you feel you have to have but that you refuse to buy immediately. Keep it wrapped around your credit card, or in your check register.

When you reach for your thirty-day list, you can trick your mind into thinking you're reaching for your money, which gives you a slight relief from the itch and reduces the urge.

In that brief moment, the part of your brain that the advertiser has a hold of relaxes a little, and you come back to reality for a moment. The reality is that you don't really want this thing, you have no conceivable use for it, but an extremely clever advertising and marketing campaign has gotten you to think you do.

Immediately write down on your thirty-day list the date and the name of the item. Put the list back in your pocket. Turn around and leave the premises posthaste.

You'll be amazed at how just being aware of the warning signs will simplify your life.

51. Come Up with a Creative Solution Rather than a Buying Solution

One of the first pieces of gear we unloaded was our exercycle.

We had purchased it a number of years before, secondhand though barely used: a big, beautiful, shiny, monolithic testament to consumer gullibility. I rode it perhaps half a dozen times; then it sat in the corner of our bedroom collecting dust, making me feel guilty every time I walked by it.

We've congratulated ourselves many times over these past few years for having had the good sense to get rid of it when we were clearing out the clutter.

Recently, after five exercise-equipment-free years of walking along the beach every morning, we started thinking that we might be able to meet our exercise needs more effectively with a different shiny, monolithic testament to consumer gullibility: a treadmill.

Our puppies provided our excuse. Over the past year our walks had gradually regressed into doggie strolls with frequent pauses while the dogs do what dogs really prefer to do on walks: sniff. Gradually, we lost the aerobic and calorie-burning benefits of our daily walks.

We still enjoyed these strolls with the dogs and the opportunity they gave us to be outdoors together, watching sunrises or sunsets and delighting in the beauty of nature.

But they weren't exercise.

So we started thinking about an alternative approach. We came across a series of ads for a treadmill that seemed to address our very problem. The seduction had begun. So, even though we should know better, we succumbed once again to the lure of the advertising dollar.

Well, we *almost* succumbed. Thanks to our thirty-day list and the fact that we'd become aware of the changes in our vital signs, we stopped ourselves in the nick of time. We'd come so close to spending money for a six-foot-long, three-foot-wide piece of plug-in equipment that provided absolutely no benefit that a slight change in our schedule wouldn't provide much more simply and at no expense.

Our solution, after resisting the urge to acquire the treadmill, was simple and obvious: We stroll once around the half-mile length of the park with the dogs for our warm-up and their sniffs, and then we take them back to the car. We increase our speed to a brisk pace and walk twice more around the park for our aerobic exercise. It's so simple.

But I'm embarrassed to confess how close we came to capitulating to a complicated and ultimately ineffective buying solution.

I mention it because I suspect there are many people, perhaps even you, who are sometimes as susceptible as we are to an effective ad campaign.

I want to point out that our solution might not necessarily be your solution. When I asked the clerk in the aerobic equipment store what the benefit of this machine was over simply getting out and walking faster, he replied: "It's the time and inclement weather displacement factor."

Meaning, if you have to spend half an hour driving to the park to walk, or if you live in Minneapolis and can't walk outdoors six months out of the year because of the weather, a treadmill might provide a simple way to get your exercise.

But since our park is only a few minutes away and we live in a climate where it rains roughly three days a year, these reasons are not relevant for us. And an expensive treadmill is not the answer for us.

Take the time to come up with other solutions to your next perceived buying need, or at the very least, wait for a few days to let the immediate gratification impulse lose its hold on you. It's so easy to end up, as many of us have, with an expensive piece of machinery that does nothing more than sit idly collecting dust, while cluttering up our lives.

52. Recognize the Point of Diminishing Returns

When we were deciding what to get rid of, our stereo and record collection were high on the list.

Even though at that point we had invested a fair amount of money in our stereo system, and even though we'd enjoyed having it, we realized that since we'd acquired our VCR we seldom listened to the stereo anymore. The reality is that we can't watch videos and listen to records or tapes at the same time. And we'd reached a point in our lives where, if we're not watching old movies, we prefer a quiet evening of reading.

Most households now have one or more television sets, one or more radios, half a dozen tape players, a video camera, a VCR, a stereo system, a CD player, several Walkmans, and a dozen computer games that fill up the space and the time that used to be taken up by a single household radio. Isn't it ironic that we're acquiring more and more goods, but have less and less time to spend with them?

But even if we had the leisure time that our parents or our grandparents had, there is a point of diminishing returns. You might want to keep this in mind the next time you're considering the acquisition of one more item that will take up time and space in your life. At the very least, consider passing on to someone else the items you'll no longer have time for.

53. When You Bring In Something New, Throw Out Something Old

I got this idea from readers. It's such a basic concept. It's so simple. And it works. You can teach it to your kids. You can easily put it into practice in your own life.

Well, it's not always so easy; but it'll definitely help you keep the clutter to manageable limits.

It applies to clothes, books, toys, shoes, tools, dishes, glassware, kitchen gadgets, computers and other electronic equipment, telephones, eyeglasses, linens, towels, pillows, umbrellas, and among other things, furniture.

Furniture? Yes. And this is the one area where most people already put this idea into practice. Given the limitations of the average home, if you purchase a new couch, more often than not you'll pass the old one on to someone else who might be able to use it. Otherwise, the living room would quickly be quite obviously overcrowded.

But in other areas of our homes, the overcrowding is not so immediately apparent. Most bookcases can hold another book. Most closets can hold another outfit. Most kitchen pantries can hold another toaster oven. Most toy boxes can hold another Barbie doll. And so forth. Up to a point.

When we go beyond that point, our stuff starts to get out of hand. If we'd started way-back-when throwing out the old when we brought in the new, we wouldn't have tool chests so jammed we can never find a screwdriver, or lingerie drawers so crammed we can never find a decent pair of knee socks, or linen closets so full of everything else that we can't open the door without having half the contents come tumbling down around our ankles.

Gibbs and I have learned to use this method to keep our books within bounds. Now, when we acquire a new book, we go through the shelves and pick an old book to pass on to someone else. We also use this system with our clothes.

It's often difficult to predict ahead of time the point at which there's too much stuff for any given space. But if you get in the habit of throwing out the old when you bring in the new, you won't have to predict. You can simply enjoy the freedom of un-cluttered spaces.

54. The Simple Souvenir

As a travel writer, Gibbs spends a good deal of time visiting interesting places around the globe.

It started to become obvious that we'd soon overload our family and friends and run out of space in our home if we continued to bring back shrunken heads from every place we visited. Aside from the expense, there was always the hassle of fitting one more thing into the luggage, maneuvering through customs, and arriving back home with the item still intact.

Early on we began keeping souvenir matchbook covers from the restaurants we visited on our travels. We now have one huge bowl that sits on our kitchen countertop that holds hundreds of matchbooks. Hardly a week goes by that one of us doesn't reach in, pull out a matchbook, read the inscription, and pull up a wonderful memory from our travels.

The Plow and Angel, the San Ysidro Ranch where we fell in love. The Three Georges, Georgetown, where we spent our honeymoon. The Pacific International Hotel, Cairns, Australia. Jumby Bay, Antigua. The Wakaya Club, Fiji Islands. Johnny Sesaws, Peru, Vermont. The Atlantic Inn, Block Island.

The matchbooks are colorful. They're lightweight. They're nonbreakable. They require no special packaging and they fit easily into a jacket pocket for the trip home. They're available everywhere. They're low maintenance. They don't need to be insured. They're functional. They're free. Eighteen years of memories that fit into a decorative bowl. The ideal souvenir for the simple life.

Other simple souvenirs that won't run you out of house and home and pocketbook include airline luggage tags, postcards, small flag insignia, or postage stamps from foreign countries.

55. What to Tell the Grandkids

Recently a woman pulled me aside after one of my speaking engagements and told me all the steps she and her husband had taken to simplify their lives. This included accepting an early retirement package offered by her husband's employer, selling their house, paring down their possessions to what would fit into their motor home, and setting out for two to three years to travel around the country to see the sights and to visit their four children and nine grandchildren who were scattered around the country.

Her problem was, what to tell the grandchildren when they asked what she and Grandpa wanted for Christmas, or birthdays, or as going away mementos.

Being supportive grandparents, they didn't want to discourage their grandchildren's creative endeavors. But they were so delighted to have reached a point where they were free of time- and energy-consuming possessions. They had exactly what they wanted, and they didn't have room in their scaled-back lifestyle to accommodate a lot of *chotchkes*, no matter how imaginative the object or well intentioned the thought behind it.

The answer seemed obvious to me: Ask for a box of home-made fudge, or a basket of Christmas cookies, or any other *consumable* items within the range of the kids' talents and their parents' patience.

A gift of this type encourages thoughtful and resource-conscious gift giving on the part of the children, while providing the grandparents with a sweet reminder of the gift bearer.

The gift would be short lived—only as long as it takes to consume a box of brownies—but the memory of it could last forever. ("Remember how delicious Sara's gingerbread men tasted that evening as we watched the sun set over the Grand Canyon?")

It wouldn't put a strain on their space limitations, nor would it ultimately be one more thing to discard into our overloaded ecosystem.

Also, it would be an excellent opportunity to propose to their children and grandchildren that the time has come in all our

lives to think about scaling back on our purchasing and consuming habits.

Gift giving doesn't have to mean going to a store to *purchase*
some item that the other person may or may not want, and may
or may not have space for. A lovingly crafted card or the joy of
quiet time spent together can add far more meaning to our lives
than a bagatelle plucked off the consumer merry-go-round.
What better way to teach succeeding generations how little we
need to be happy.

And what better legacy to leave our kids than a new consumer
ethic.

56. Put a Moratorium on Shopping

In Chapter Two, I mention that one way to save time is to limit your purchases over the next thirty days to groceries and basic essentials.

This practice has several obvious benefits. Not only will it save you time and money and minimize the clutter, but it will go a long way toward changing your consuming habits.

When Gibbs and I looked at the process we'd gone through to eliminate the stuff we no longer wanted in our lives, we saw that we'd made some fairly wise choices. We had minimized our stuff, and there wasn't much more we needed or wanted to acquire.

Even so, we found ourselves falling into some of our old buying patterns. Since we'd had such great success with our thirty-day list (#49), we decided to take that idea a step further. As an experiment, we put a moratorium on shopping. We decided we wouldn't purchase anything except groceries and personal necessities for three months.

If we began to feel there was something we might want to acquire, we'd either put it on a list for later or we'd come up with a creative solution rather than a buying solution (#51).

Going for three months without shopping for anything but our food and personal items turned out to be so liberating we extended the moratorium for another three months.

This was not about living in austerity or depriving ourselves of the things we need. We approached it as a challenge and an opportunity to break the buying habits that had been a force in our lives. Not only did we save time and money and reduce the clutter that comes into our home, but we drastically changed our consumer mentality. We simply don't acquire stuff like we used to.

When you look at the buying habits that have taken hold in our culture over the past thirty years or so, you can see that we made the decision somewhere along the line to work longer hours so we could acquire more things. We've exchanged our leisure time for stuff.

A lot of us are starting to question that exchange. It hasn't been a good trade-off. Not for us, not for our children, not for the environment.

I urge you to try this moratorium. Even if you do it for only thirty days it'll be an eye-opener. You'll see how little we really need, and how easy it is to get along without most of the things we feel we have to have.

Learning to step off the consumer treadmill has been one of the major benefits Gibbs and I have gotten from simplifying our lives.

SEVEN

Learning to
Say No

57. The Truly Free Person

The playwright Jules Renard once said the truly free person is one who can turn down an invitation to dinner without giving an excuse.

It's difficult to imagine anyone actually doing that, and it's impossible for most of us to imagine doing it ourselves. In our culture it's more socially acceptable to be nice than it is to be honest or direct.

The social pressure to automatically say yes to invitations is a challenging one to overcome. There are so many considerations, and they're all mixed in together. At one level we're afraid the other person will feel rejected. At another level we're afraid that if we start saying no, people will reject us. And even though we may not want to go, there's frequently a part of us that wants to be included.

More often than not, our true desire to not accept an invitation has less to do with the invitation we'd like to decline, and more to do with our need or desire to do something else—such as spend time with our kids or a quiet evening with our partner.

But for many, it seems easier to spend an evening having dinner with people we'd rather not have dinner with than it is to put up with the guilt or the discomfort we'd feel if we turned down the invitation in the first place.

Then there are all the shoulds. It's obvious there are some things we feel we should do—like taking care of an ailing parent or helping a friend in need, among others—that we really should do. But there are often many things we feel we should do that, in fact, we don't really have to do. Getting to the point where we can tell the difference is a major milestone in the simplification process.

For some fortunate people this is not a problem. But for many the inability to graciously decline an invitation, or to stop doing all the things they feel they should do, is a major complication. It robs us of many hours we could spend doing something we'd rather do.

As you begin to simplify your life, you're going to be making a lot of changes in the way you spend your time. If saying no is a problem for you, go back to your short list (#21) and keep it firmly in mind. Your objective will be to get to the point where you see that by turning down an invitation you're not saying no to someone else; rather you're saying yes! to what you really want to do.

58. One Way to Deal with the Guilt of Saying No

One woman who attended a talk I gave suggested the following solution to the problem of social invitations and the guilt that often accompanies our desire to say no.

She'd been in the travel business for many years and had finally reached a point where she was fed up with constantly being on the go and feeling she had to say yes to every invitation that came across her desk.

When she first started out, she loved the social whirl. It gave her a chance to meet new people and to expand not only her social base but her client base as well. Over the years, both hosting and attending dinner meetings and cocktail parties became an integral part of her life.

But in recent years it had gotten to be too much. She realized she no longer knew where her business life ended and her personal life began.

She decided she needed a breather. So she stopped issuing and accepting social invitations entirely for six months. She said that what made it so easy—and eliminated the guilt—was that she said no to everyone, no exceptions.

Obviously, this freed up a lot of her time, which she used to evaluate where she was in her life. By stopping everything she had a chance to see that she was ready to make some changes in her career. She'd been moving so fast, she was unaware that she was close to burnout.

At the end of six months, she sold her business and moved across the country to start working for a small travel magazine where she could use and develop her writing talents.

Your desire to reduce the number of social activities in your life may have nothing to do with a career move, but you can still use her tactic. Simply decline any and all invitations for a month or two or more. The time you free up could provide a lot of clarity and direction for your life.

If you keep this plan in place long enough, the invitations may stop coming in altogether. This will give you a chance to clean the slate, and perhaps to start all over again. You might choose to do it differently next time.

59. Move Beyond the Guilt

Like many people, I used to have a problem with the guilt of saying no. And sometimes I still do.

But my friend, Sue, is much more realistic about dealing with invitations. Her philosophy has helped me eliminate a lot of the guilt that comes from saying no.

She points out that the one who's doing the asking might like you to join them, but if you don't accept the invitation, it won't be the end of the world for them. Someone else will accept, or they'll make other plans, so it's no big deal.

Now, they may *say* it's a big deal. After all, that's the socially acceptable thing to do—what else can one who's extending an invitation do if someone declines, say they're *glad* you're not coming? It's just not done.

So they make regretful noises ("So sorry you can't join us...maybe next time...we'll miss you" and the like). And usually they're sincere, but they're probably not devastated. Those kinds of comments were designed to get everyone off the hook gracefully, not to induce guilt in the one who is declining.

And so the one who gets declined moves on, and they don't think a whole lot about it. In truth, they're too busy getting on with their life or tracking down the next person on their list to hold your no against you. But certainly any momentary flash of regret a host might feel because someone declines is seldom worth the paroxysms of guilt felt by the one who's declining.

After all, when someone turns you down, you don't rush to the nearest cliff to leap off. No. You move on. Though you probably say things like you're so sorry they can't join you, you'll miss them, maybe next time, and you usually mean it. But you probably don't think enough about it to justify the guilt they might feel by saying no to you.

Also, keep in mind that you're not doing anyone a favor by showing up for a dinner party or any other type of gathering when your heart isn't in it. You'd be doing the host and everyone else a much greater service by staying home and freeing up the space for someone who'd love to be there.

60. Afraid You'll Miss Something?

I was talking to my cousin, Joanie, a while back about the issue of saying no. She and her husband, Joe, had just gone through a brief soul-searching exercise because they'd recently decided they'd been going out too much, and yet they kept finding themselves saying yes to invitations that they really didn't want to accept. When they thought more about it, they realized they were saying yes because they were afraid if they didn't go, they'd miss something.

So they'd go, and invariably they'd find that what they missed out on was a quiet, restful evening at home.

I knew exactly what she meant, because I've often felt that way, too. She said she'd always thought it was a family thing—because everyone in our family feels this way.

But I know from the letters I get and the people I talk to around the country, there are many others who have this problem, too. It's a cultural thing. There are so many opportunities out there, and we don't want to miss any of them. So we frequently find ourselves in the classic dilemma of wanting to go and not wanting to go at the same time.

I've finally reached a point where I know I have to be ready to miss some new things, if only so that I'll then have time to enjoy the old things.

61. The Reality of the Urgent Request

Gibbs, who has been an active volunteer for numerous organizations over the years, recently received a card from a group he used to do volunteer work for. On it was a very gracious handwritten note from the director of the group, telling him how much they had missed him and asking him to come back to join them as soon as he could.

Since he's actively involved with a different volunteer organization right now, he knew he couldn't commit to another assignment, but the friendly note gave him a moment's pause, and just a twang of guilt. Maybe he *should* go back and help.

But after he'd thought about it for a bit, he realized the card asking him to come back was merely a routine. His name just happened to come to the top of the list. This doesn't mean they wouldn't love to have him come back, but this was a call to reactivate volunteers, not a device to make anyone feel guilty if they couldn't participate.

The need to fill a spot also applies to many social and work-related requests as well. Keep this in mind the next time someone says you simply must join them (for something you're not interested in), that it just won't be the same without you. It won't, but they'll survive. And so will you.

Another area that is frequently a problem for people are the social functions, or any kind of an event, that people feel they *should* attend because someone has gone to so much trouble to put them on.

My feeling is that if someone has gone to a lot of trouble to put them on, they presumably did it because they enjoy doing that type of thing. There'll be enough people who show up because they want to be there, so you don't need to feel *you* have to.

Of course, if no one shows up at all, perhaps it's an indication that the gathering wasn't necessary in the first place.

62. How to Say No

Unless you're Jules Renard, how you respond to requests for your time depends to some extent on your relationship with the person who's asking.

With friends, just be honest. "Look, I'm simplifying my life right now, and I need to slow down. I'm not going to be going out as much as I have been. It's nothing personal, but I need some time to recharge my batteries."

When a new personal or business acquaintance suggests, "Hey! Let's do lunch sometime!" nip it in the bud. You can casually say you're not doing lunch these days and leave it at that. You don't need to get into a major discussion about it.

To the crazy-makers—the mother-in-law, the next-door neighbor, the hangers-on who are always creating havoc in your life and eating up the time you'd like to spend doing other things—you may simply have to get tough. Put your foot down. And keep putting it down until they get the picture. "Blanche, I'm starting a new project next week and won't be able to do coffee with you for a while. I'll give you a call when my schedule frees up."

When Blanche shows up anyway, be firm and persistent. "Blanche, maybe I didn't make myself clear the other day, but remember I'm starting my new schedule today. I don't have time to visit now. I'll call you later."

If it's someone you feel you *should* see, then set some parameters. "I'm available on Friday afternoon between one and two to see you," for example. But don't let them take over your life. To do this you may have to let go of your desire to be "nice." You can please some of the people some of the time, but you can't please them all, all of the time.

To requests for volunteer efforts you're not ready for yet, again, a simple explanation with a minimum of details is best. "Sorry. I don't have the time now. I'll call you when my schedule clears up."

For any other situations where you know you need to say no, be inventive. This is your life you're making time for.

63. Saying No in the Workplace

You may not have a problem saying no in social situations, but you might be a pushover at work. In *The Overworked American*, Harvard sociologist Juliet Schor reports that many fast trackers have continued to work longer and longer hours without a corresponding increase in pay because they don't know how to say no.

Somehow, in the workplace, corporate management has gotten us to believe that saying no to more work and longer hours is tantamount to being un-American. And there's always the fear that if we don't say yes to whatever time-demanding project is passed our way, someone else will, and we'll be without a job or won't get that next promotion.

Saying no to the boss. Ah, that's a tough one. There's so much at stake—namely our livelihood. If you're simplifying your life, there are other areas where you can free up time and energy which may help you put up with, for the time being, a demanding job that requires, or that you feel requires, long hours.

But this is simply another area where you may have to learn to say no. According to Professor Schor, a number of recent studies have shown that workers *are* starting to say no to longer hours. Many people are moving away from the frenzied work ethic of the 1980s to more traditional values.

Professor Schor points out, however, that shorter work schedules won't be handed over to us by management. Rather, we'll have to claim them for ourselves.

If you're tired of working ten- and twelve-hour days, reduce your workday by half an hour or more over the next couple of months. No one's going to miss you for that half hour. Besides, you may be amazed to find, as I did, that you're more productive when you're working less. You'll therefore be making more of a contribution. You can then cut back even more.

Your next challenge might be deciding how to spend your extra time. After you recuperate—with rest, quiet time, long walks, time in nature, time with your family, time at the movies, —check out your creative urges. You will be pleasantly surprised at what's been cooking away inside all this time.

64. So Why Haven't You Written Your Book?

Or painted your Mona Lisa? Or sculpted your David? Or written your play, or started any of the other creative pursuits you have in the back of your mind that you'd like to do?

We all have creative ideas we want to develop. We may have been too busy to explore them, or we may have believed they were impossible for us to do. But it's our heart's desire that we should be doing.

Ask anyone who's following their muse. That's when they're truly happy, that's when they're in love, that's when they have passion in their life. They do it because they heard the call. And they heard the call because they took the time to listen.

Georgia O'Keeffe once said that it takes time to see a flower. It also takes time to write a poem. It takes time to open up to our creativity. And that time has to be free of many of the distractions we so often allow to take over our lives, often because we haven't learned to say no.

In my experience the creative process works like a locomotive. It takes a tremendous amount of inner resources and energy to start the wheels moving, and they move very slowly at first. If something on the track stops the train, it takes a tremendous amount of energy to get it going again. But once it's going full bore, it takes a lot to stop it.

When I started writing, for example, I found that I couldn't write and do lunch at the same time. By the time I get up and running, if I stop for lunch, the writing is all over for the day. After years in the real estate business, where doing lunch was de rigueur, I had to change my practices and start saying no to luncheons and many other invitations. I simplified my work life so I could expand into my creativity.

If you've got a creative project that you'd like to begin, I urge you to learn to say no to as many of the social and cultural and consumer distractions as you possibly can, so you can begin to build up the steam you need to move forward with it.

EIGHT

Some Inner Stuff

65. One Reason We're Craving Simpler Lives

Dear Ms. St. James;

I am 14 years old, and this school year I will be in ninth grade. About two years ago, I started feeling like my life was missing something. At first I thought I was lonely. I would get sick and lie in bed and cry. Loneliness didn't really make sense though. My parents love me. I have a brother I get along with. I have a dog, and I have friends I can talk to and trust. Then, about a year ago, my parents sent me to a psychiatrist. I only went four or five times, and I didn't feel helped. But a few months ago I decided that I didn't have to feel so depressed all the time. I pulled myself out of my pit of despair. I am still pulling. I give myself pep talks when I need them. When I am angry, I climb a large tree in my backyard. I feel that I am making progress.

I finished your book *Inner Simplicity* about ten minutes ago. I now realize that I am lonely, but not for company. I am lonely for myself. All my life so far I have concentrated on school, and being good, and being other people's idea of perfect. But now I know that I need to not worry so much about what others think but to do things I like to do. I need to look inside myself for strength. I need to get in touch with my inner self. I want to thank you for helping me realize that. I plan to try everything in your book, and to read the books you recommended.

Very sincerely,
Erin Webreck
Somerset, PA

"I am lonely for myself."

Erin speaks eloquently for many of us. We've been so busy being the good wife, the good husband, the good mother, the good father, the good son, the good daughter, the outstanding employee, the successful entrepreneur, and everyone else's idea of what perfect is that we've lost touch with who we really are.

As you begin living a simpler life, you'll have the time to spend in solitude, to write in your journal, to get some counseling if you feel the need, to work on eliminating any addictions that may be getting in your way, to learn to forgive, to develop gratitude, to figure out your big issue, and to learn how to move through your life at a pace that allows you to enjoy each day to the fullest.

Go back to Chapter Two and take another look at some things you might do to free up some time to think about simplifying your life (#13, #14, #15, and #16).

Another benefit of having this newfound time will be the opportunity to begin to get reacquainted with yourself.

66. Why We Keep Our Lives So Hectic

One thing I've learned about maintaining a complicated life is that it's one of the best ways we have to avoid looking at some of the larger questions. It may not apply to everyone, but I believe it explains a lot about why we've been moving so fast. The prospect of getting reacquainted with ourselves can be daunting.

As long as we convince ourselves that we're so busy and our work is so vital and we can't afford to slow down, then we don't have to look at our own lives and the personal issues that are so difficult to address: a marriage that isn't working, a career that isn't satisfying, children we're out of touch with, friendships we've outgrown, associations we need to move on from, the creativity we've been afraid to explore, our deepest fears or childhood traumas that have been holding us back from leading truly fulfilled lives.

As you start to slow down, to cut back your work hours, and

to free yourself from some of your commitments, you're going to have some time on your hands.

To begin with you may feel the need to start nourishing your body by catching up on your sleep, cleaning up your eating patterns, restoring your energy, reestablishing an exercise regimen, spending some time in nature, learning how to laugh and how to have fun.

And then gradually, you may reach a point where there's nothing left to do but start to deal with some of those inner issues. With a blanket of time around you, you'll find they're not as monumental as they may once have seemed. Creating the inner strength to move through them will lighten you up.

An amazing thing happens when we slow down. We start to get flashes of inspiration. We reach a new level of understanding and even wisdom. In a quiet moment we can get an intuitive insight that can change our entire life and the lives of the people around us in incredibly positive ways. And those changes can last a lifetime.

Living more simply will make it possible to create those quiet moments. Out of those quiet moments miracles happen. Be open to them.

67. Find Your Life's Work

One of the greatest benefits I've derived from simplifying my life has been finding a new and satisfying career. I wish I could say it was easy. It wasn't. It was one of the biggest challenges I've ever had to meet. But as anyone knows who is doing something they truly love to do, there is nothing like it, and few things they would exchange for it.

I spent most of my life not knowing what I wanted to do when I grew up. I've taken a lot of the tests, I've read many of the books, I've talked to numerous career counselors. But the only career guidance that worked for me was the advice to take some time off and do nothing until I figured out what my next career move should be.

Perhaps the hardest part was coming to the decision that I could take the time off. As we know, when we're in the middle of a hectic life, we think we can't stop. But slowing down makes it possible to see many options that simply aren't apparent when we're moving at warp speed.

The next hardest part was figuring out how to arrange it financially. I've already mentioned *Your Money or Your Life* by Joe Dominguez and Vicki Robin. Their approach to achieving financial independence gave me an entirely new way of thinking about the time and effort it takes to earn the money we spend. And of course, if you're living more simply you'll be spending significantly less money in the process.

If you're considering taking steps to find your life's work, and finances are one of your considerations, I urge you to study some or all of the money books described on the Reading List. You'll find an almost unlimited number of ways to reduce your expenses or to rearrange your finances so you can explore new career options.

Once you put your mind to it, you'll begin to see that saying you can't afford to find a more satisfying career is only an excuse. It's the most deceptive excuse there is. The truth is, in terms of the quality of your life, you can't afford *not* to.

Once I moved beyond the excuses, I made the commitment

to myself that I wouldn't start anything new until I came up with something I wanted to do. Out of that commitment I started writing, just for the fun of it and because I loved doing it. It opened up new career possibilities for me that I never would have thought of if I hadn't made that promise and stuck to it.

Though Gibbs and I did a lot of rearranging so I could take some time off, you may not have to do that. I'm a slow learner. I had to completely change my pace before I could begin to ask the right questions. Then I had to listen for the answers.

Don't fall into the trap of thinking that if you're not now doing what you love to do, it's too late to figure it out. One thing I've realized is that everything I did previously prepared me for what I'm doing now. And what I'm doing now is no doubt preparing me for whatever I may do differently in the future.

With the rapid changes that are happening in the market-place, with the downshifting that's happening in the work-place with the increasing advances in all phases of technology, there perhaps has never been a better time to figure out what your best work is, if only as preparation for the next stage of your life.

If you're not doing work you love, the greatest contribution you can make to the world and to your own growth is to *take whatever time you need to figure out what you want to do.* Then start doing it.

68. Giving Back

Across the country, volunteer organizations have reported a significant decline over the past decade in the numbers of people who are willing to devote time to charitable or other worthy causes. Our ten- and twelve-hour workdays have not left much time for volunteer endeavors.

But as simplifying and downshifting take hold in this culture, the numbers of people who are ready to give back will start to rise again. I hear from many readers that one of the major benefits of simplifying their lives is that now they have time to devote to others through volunteering.

One reader said, "My own view is that getting out of the rat race through simplifying solves only half of the problem of lack of fulfilment that so many people experience. The other half is found in considering the needs of others as much as our own."

Volunteering may not be high on your short list as you begin to simplify your life. If you're feeling exhausted and depleted from the frenetic pace of your life in recent years, perhaps it shouldn't be. Charity begins at home. It's possible that one of the greatest services you can perform is to get your own house in shape and to spend time with your kids and your spouse and your extended family before you rush out to save the world.

But the time may soon come when you're ready to give back. Doing something for others can be a very powerful step toward getting to know yourself and for adding joy and value and a sense of accomplishment to your life. The distinguished historian Arnold Toynbee said that the future of mankind depends on every person withdrawing into himself and finding his own depths, then coming forth to serve his fellow men.

And remember, your greatest service and where you can make the greatest contribution is when you're doing what you love to do (#67).

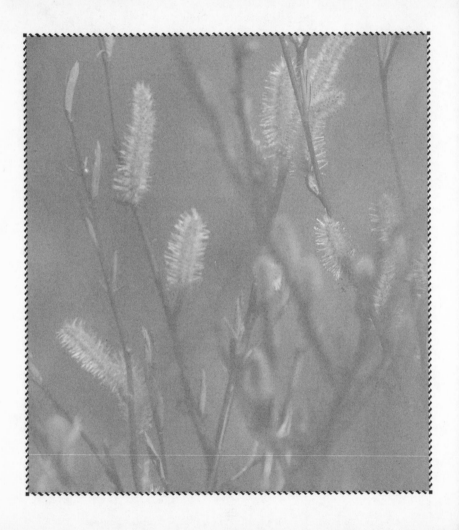

NINE

Personal and Household Routines

69. Another Approach to Household Chores

Several readers of *Simplify Your Life* wrote to say they had learned to spread out the weekly routines into more easily manageable portions that take less time.

Margo Bogart of Dearborn, Michigan, put it this way:

"I have streamlined my household chores by having a major focus for each day of the week. This may sound trite, but it actually saves me the trouble of trying to remember how long it has been since I last did each major task. Each person can vary the concept to suit his or her needs and flex the schedule when circumstances require switching days for certain tasks. Here's my basic plan:

Monday: empty wastebaskets and put out trash for city garbage pickup. Do laundry.

Tuesday: Work on computer. Clean second floor and basement.

231

Wednesday: Volunteer. Shop on the way home.

Thursday: Clean bathrooms.

Friday: Vacuum carpets and mop floors. Plan activities to do together for the weekend.

Saturday: Spend as much time together as possible. If my husband brings work home from the office, I pay bills, write letters, clip coupons, dust, iron, mend, water plants, etc., until we can spend more time together.

Sunday: Work in the yard and garden together or do repairs together. Phone relatives together. Relax and read together.

"This system works for me. It's true that I don't have the best kept house in Dearborn, but I think I have one of the happiest marriages! The beauty of having a preestablished focus for each day of the week is that I never waste time trying to figure out what I should be accomplishing next.

"Also, this schedule helps me pace myself and not feel like I'm falling behind when responsibilities threaten to pile up. Once I have done the designated chores for the day, I feel more comfortable about allocating time for other tasks (or invitations to do fun things!) that come up unexpectedly. I feel more in control of my week and less stressed by the endless 'to-do' list."

As Margo says, such a plan can be adapted to your own circumstances.

Another reader said she completed one household task before she headed for the office each morning. This way, she didn't have to think about doing it at the end of her workday when she was tired and would thus be more inclined to skip it. She also pointed out that it meant she didn't have to lose a major part of her weekend to the drudgery of chores, and instead she looked forward all week to being able to spend her Saturday doing whatever she wanted to do.

70. A Simple Weekly Menu Plan

Though Gibbs and I both love to eat, neither one of us wants to spend a lot of time in the kitchen. So years ago we came up with a solution to the perennial question, "What are we having for dinner tonight?"

We didn't recognize how much it simplified our lives until I started hearing it as a tip from readers who do it, too. I know this won't work for everyone, and it's a flagrant violation of the get off automatic pilot suggestion (#30), but we got into the habit of eating pretty much the same thing each night of the week.

For example, on Mondays we have grilled chicken breasts with steamed veggies.

On Tuesdays we usually eat at one of our favorite local restaurants.

On Wednesdays we have either a large Greek salad or a salade Niçoise with one of Gibbs's muffins.

On Thursdays we have fresh crab or tuna gazpacho with a muffin in summer—or a hot veggie soup in winter. Or sometimes we really break loose and have grilled chicken with veggies again.

On Fridays we have Gibbs's scrambled eggs with whole wheat toast, turkey sausage, and fresh squeezed orange juice.

We like to keep it light on the weekends, so on Saturdays (our favorite) we have blue corn tortilla chips with fresh guacamole.

On Sundays we have popcorn and apples with cheese. This leaves room for our weekend dessert treat, maybe a fresh fruit cobbler or berries and cream.

We'll stick with this menu until we get tired of it; then we'll come up with another menu plan. As one reader pointed out, this simplifies not only the meal planning, but also the grocery list, the shopping, the provisioning, the cooking, and the cleanup. It's one less thing to have to occupy your mind with each day.

Another reader told me about a variation on this theme, which Ethel Kennedy has reportedly used for years: a menu plan based on simple roasts and broiled meats, omelets, and salads that rotates every two weeks instead of each week.

I know that for many people this approach would be boring beyond belief. Obviously, if you love to cook, you can do other things to simplify your life so you have the time to spend preparing your favorite meals.

But Gibbs and I enjoy knowing each morning what we're going to have for dinner that night. We eat only foods we're really fond of, so we tend to look forward all day to our predictable dinners.

71. Some Other Possibilities for Simple Meals

This idea, which I heard from many readers, is one I did for years: Cook up a week's supply of spaghetti sauce or lasagne or one of your favorite soups or casseroles, freeze it in meal-sized portions so it doesn't spoil, and have it every night for a week, perhaps with a different salad or a variety of rolls or fresh bread.

I recently came across another book that you might explore if the idea of cooking ahead and freezing appeals to you: *Once a Month Cooking* by Mimi Wilson and Mary Beth Lagerboard. It's a step-by-step guide for preparing a month's worth of dinner entrees in advance and freezing them.

Depending on the size of your family, the program might require the addition of some larger cooking pots, extra freezer space, and a lot of organization. And it definitely requires a complete day of your time each month to do the menu plan, the provisioning, and the cooking. If you're willing to put in that whole day, it would definitely save you money and simplify your life.

Another simple option for frozen meals might be Healthy Choice or Lean Cuisine or any of the other well-balanced, dietetically proportioned frozen dinners that are now available. These are not the standard TV dinners. A friend recommended these to us a while back and we found, to our surprise, that they are quite delicious. If you select carefully, you can find a variety that are well balanced in terms of protein, carbohydrates, and fat and the appropriate micronutrients.

Gibbs and I keep some of these on hand for evenings when we don't want to go out to eat and want the simplest meal possible. Yes, they are more expensive than using Mimi and Mary Beth's system of cooking from scratch and then freezing, but as a stopgap measure—and with the addition of a fresh salad— they're another simple solution.

And given that the major cause of overweight in this country is overeating, an added benefit we've found from having this type of frozen dinner from time to time is that it's a very simple way to limit our food intake. The preset portions serve as an excellent reminder of how little we need to eat to stay fit and healthy.

72. A Simple Way to Maintain Your Weight

I don't believe everyone needs to be pencil thin. But I have found that life is simpler if I can keep my weight to what for me is an acceptable level. When I do, I feel better, I look better, and I don't have to keep a thin wardrobe and a heavy wardrobe in my closet.

Gibbs and I have struggled for years with the problem of maintaining our ideal weight. A couple of years ago we discovered what has become for us a surefire way to keep our weight in check: We use a chart to track our weight each day.

We use plain graph paper taped to the wall above the bathroom scales, and we keep a red pen nearby.

It's amazing how easy it is to nip in the bud a small weight gain from a dinner out, or some indiscriminate snacking from the day before, when we're keeping track on a daily basis. If we're up a pound in the morning, we know we have to make some adjustment in our intake for the rest of the day in order to bring it back down by the next morning, or possibly the next.

Modifying our food intake based on the movement of that red line up the graph becomes an automatic, unconscious, and almost painless way to maintain the weight we want.

Time and again, if we slack off on using the chart—either we've been too lazy to make up a new one for the month or we've misplaced the pen—we can gain five pounds without batting an eye. It's so easy to convince ourselves that the piece of double chocolate mousse cake was only a small piece, or that the extra handful of M&Ms we pilfered at last night's meeting didn't count because we ate them standing up. But the chart isn't so easily convinced.

We've found it's not sufficient simply to weigh in every morning and not mark the weight on the graph. If we do that, we somehow conveniently forget what we weighed the day before and the day before that. But it's impossible to lose track when the weight is recorded in bright red ink on the bathroom wall, and difficult to ignore when it's moving inexorably up the graph.

Now we photocopy enough weight graphs to last the entire year, and we keep the red pen in a nearby drawer so it doesn't get misplaced. Maintain your ideal weight with a red pen. It's so simple.

73. Dealing with Unwanted Callers

Margo Bogart also had some good ideas for dealing with incoming phone calls and uninvited solicitors at the front door.

She says, "Our first line of defense against unwanted phone interruptions at home is an unlisted number. The reduction in dinner-time interruptions has been well worth the onetime $40 cost of switching from a listed to an unlisted number. Now all the people we want to hear from have our number, and most of those who would solicit us for purchases or contributions don't.

"Also, to keep your number out of the computer files of businesses with Caller ID, we begin by pressing *67 before we press the phone number. This defeats the Caller ID system, but only for that call, so we must remember to press *67 whenever we call an organization we don't necessarily want to hear from later. I've put a sticker on my telephone receiver to remind us to use this blocking code more often. (The blocking code number varies from region to region, depending on your phone service provider.)

"For those telephone solicitors who make it through our first line of defense, I have a foolproof response that brings their calls to a speedy conclusion. Years ago my husband and I made a pact to simplify our lives: We will not buy from any salesperson or contribute to any cause that approaches us by phone (or at our front door). This pact leaves no room for the salesperson to attempt to change our minds, so it really is foolproof. I simply say, 'Sorry, we don't accept any telephone offers,' or 'We don't contribute to any organizations through telephone solicitations.' My husband's response is even simpler: 'NO, thank you.' (Click.)

"Regarding your suggestion about not answering the doorbell, either, we have saved ourselves untold visits from the area Fuller Brush man, religious proselytizers, and kids selling candy and magazine subscriptions by posting a hand-lettered sign in plain sight near our front doorbell. It reads: 'No Soliciting. We don't do business at our front door.' As persistent as these callers are trained to be, they generally remove themselves from our front porch without even ringing or knocking when they see our sign."

A big part of learning to say no (#62) is learning to avoid the kinds of situations that put you in the position of refusing a request. If this is a problem in your neighborhood or in your life, preparing for them in advance will help. In life as in football the best defense is often a good offense.

74. The Simple Answering Machine

We all know about using the answering machine to screen phone calls and about turning the phone off altogether if we need some uninterrupted time to work or spend time with our kids.

But I've found another effective way to utilize this true time-saving device. An associate and I keep in touch via our answering machines.

Monica and I know that if we get on the phone together, we can talk for ages. That's fine when we both have the time, but our lives are such now that one or the other of us is always on a deadline. So we agreed some years back that when one of us has some information to pass on to the other, we'll just leave a message on the machine.

Even if the other person is there and listening to the message as it's coming in, neither one of us has to feel compelled to pick up the phone. In fact, often we prefer that the other not pick up.

And so the one calling will say, "If you're there, don't pick up, but I just wanted you to know such and such."

If the other party has a need to respond to the message, she can then call back and leave any pertinent information on the other's machine.

I have since established similar answering machine relationships with people I have no need to talk to in person, but whom I have a need to keep in touch with. Think of it as audio E-mail.

Obviously, this arrangement wouldn't work for all your relationships, but learning to use the telephone effectively can free up an extrordinary amount of time that you might not even be aware you're losing.

Another way to keep incoming phone calls under control is simply to let people know when it's convenient to call you. If you want to avoid phone interruptions during your mealtime, have all the family members let their friends and associates know that they can reach you before 6 p.m. or after 7 p.m. or whenever your dinner slot is, and that any calls during that time will not be picked up.

Another option is to set up a phone date. Arrange, even through answering machine messages if necessary, to get together by phone at a prespecified time.

But perhaps one of the greatest advantages to having an answering machine pick up your calls is that telemarketers will hang up when a machine answers.

75. The Simple Fireplace

If you're a purist when it comes to wood-burning fires, please don't read this.

But if you are tired of the hassle of wood-burning fires and have access to natural gas, consider installing a gas-burning log in your existing hearth.

Gibbs and I love sitting quietly in front of a fire on a cold evening. But, except for special occasions, we went for years without enjoying our fireplace because of the inconvenience involved.

To begin with, unless you have your own source of wood, there's the expense and the bother of having the wood delivered to the house and stacked in a suitable place, away from the house to avoid termites, but not so far away that it's a bother to retrieve the logs when you need them.

Then you have to haul the wood—free of spiders and other

insects—into the house and build the fire, cleaning up the bits of bark and chipped wood as you go. Then you've got to get the fire lit and keep it burning without smoking out the living room in the process. You've got to make certain the fire screen is in place so that flying sparks don't burn holes in the carpet after you've gone to bed.

At some point you've got to clean out all the ash from the burned wood, and depending on how much wood you use through the season, you should have the chimney cleaned at least once a year.

Unless you particularly enjoy chopping wood, having a gas log means you can eliminate that chore from your list or cancel your standing order for wood for the winter.

Admittedly, Gibbs and I live in a mild climate, and though we wouldn't be able to do this if we lived in Wisconsin, we use our gas log through most of the heating season as our only source of heat for our home. The recent technological advances in ceramic logs have not only made gas-burning logs much more realistic looking and attractive, they're much more efficient as well. We light the fire early in the evening, let it burn for an hour or so, and then turn it off. Because of the heat-storing capability of the logs, it will continue to put out heat for at least another hour or more. Of course, we also keep sweaters and extra blankets nearby during the colder months.

Burning a gas log is considerably cheaper than burning wood, running roughly a quarter to a third the expense, depending on where you live. Best of all, gas burns much cleaner and is more environmentally friendly than burning wood.

Though a gas fire doesn't have that wonderful snap and crackle that a wood fire has, and you don't get the wood-burning aroma, we've found a gas fire is just as warm and just as romantic as a wood fire, much easier, and you never have to interrupt a cozy snuggle to stoke the logs.

76. The Simple Bed

Gibbs is a churner. He falls asleep easily and sleeps soundly, but tosses from one side to the other all night long, taking the covers with him at every turn.

It takes me a few minutes to get the covers and the pillow adjusted comfortably, but then I fall asleep and remain in exactly the same position until morning.

Gibbs is a heat machine and needs only a light cover. I'm usually cold at night and like a heavy quilt.

The standard bed with sheets and blankets tucked in at the bottom doesn't work for our different sleeping habits. After years of struggling, Gibbs and I have finally devised a much simpler way for each of us to get a good night's sleep.

Though it might not work for every couple with radically different sleeping habits, our solution to this common problem works well for us, and several readers wrote to describe variations on our approach to the simple bed.

We have a king-sized bed with a fitted sheet over the mattress. We each have a queen-sized comforter. Mine is heavyweight; Gibbs's is lightweight.

We fold each comforter in half—the lightweight one goes on his side of the bed and the heavyweight one goes on my side—and we use them as sleeping bags. The folded edge of each comforter runs down the center of the bed; the open edges run down the outside edge of the bed so they're easy to get into and out of.

Because the comforters are queen size, there's plenty of room for each of us to spread out within our own quilted envelope, and it holds the heat better than a blanket spread over the whole bed.

Making the bed up in the morning is a snap. You can either leave the top half of the "bag" in casual disarray, or with one flip of the top layer, each half of the bed is neatly made (well, sort of neatly made). Several couples I heard from who use this method fold up the comforters and place them on the foot of the bed each morning.

Also, by flipping the whole arrangement head to foot or inside out, the options for irregular laundering are greatly expanded. Let your conscience be your guide. Each comforter makes a full load for the standard-sized washer and dryer.

This system makes snuggling together more of a challenge, but it keeps the game interesting.

77. Simple Laundering Ideas

It was a relief to learn that Gibbs and I were not the only ones for whom socks have been a daily and weekly complication.

Not only are they a pain in the neck to find in a freshly laundered load of clothes (mine invariably find their way down a long dark sleeve or pant leg, or into the deepest recess of a pillowcase), but then you've got to find the mate and somehow tie them together so that when you want to wear them they'll both be in roughly the same vicinity in your chest of drawers.

Finally, in self-defense, I came up with a solution that works for us. Many people have written to me with variations on this approach, so this system can be adapted to suit your own circumstances.

I bought seven identical pairs of dark socks for each of us, one pair for each day of the week.

I also bought two zippered mesh bags for each of us. The bags are available at most hardware or variety stores.

Arrange the bags side by side in your closet on a hanger or on a hook, or designate a sock drawer that will hold both bags. Fill one bag with clean socks. Since the socks are identical, you don't have to mate them. When you need a clean pair, take them from the clean bag. When you remove your socks at the end of the day, put them in the other bag. At the end of the week, toss the dirty sock bag into the laundry.

When it comes out of the dryer, it now becomes the clean bag, and the process starts all over again. You'll never have to match socks or hunt for the mate to your favorite pair again.

In terms of the rest of the laundry, several people wrote to say they never buy any launderable item in red because it *always* runs, even after many washings. I stopped buying red many years ago for this very reason.

And many people shared this idea about cutting drying time in half, which I'd never heard of before, but I now do regularly: Run your clothes through the dryer only long enough to get out the wrinkles (ten to twenty minutes, depending on the items and the dryer and the setting). Then hang them on hangers in your closet to dry completely.

This won't work for every climate, but if you can do it, not only will it save you time and reduce either the gas or electricity used by your dryer, it also eliminates wrinkles, which eliminates ironing. It also reduces the damage and wear and tear to your clothes that are caused by extended exposure to high temperatures.

Then you can get rid of your iron.

Another great laundering tip I got from readers is to use laundry disks (available from Real Goods Trading Corporation, 555 Leslie Street, Ukiah, CA 95482 (800) 762-7325).

These are 2 1/2-inch-diameter disks filled with ionizing ceramic beads. You just toss them into the washer with a load of clothes and they eliminate the need for harsh detergents—in your clothes and down the drain. They also eliminate the rapid fading of dark colors that comes from using detergents with whiteners. They are recommended for everyday washing, but do require warm water. I've used them for over a year now and find them very effective for cleaning, though I do use a teaspoon or so of detergent when I launder our dusty trail-hiking clothes.

They come in a set of three disks for $49 and last for between 500 to 700 laundry loads (roughly two years for most people).

TEN

Lifestyle Issues

78. The Simple Computer

Frequently, people ask me, "Did you get rid of your computer when you simplified your life?"

I always explain that using a computer saves me untold hours and is a tremendous simplifier for me as a writer. I can't imagine being without one.

I began to realize that people who ask this question are of the "simplifying means getting rid of everything and moving to the cabin in the woods" mind-set.

But it's a fair question. Given the rapid pace of the technological advances that are taking place every day, we're all going to have to address the issue of whether or not the computer— and the Internet, E-mail, virtual reality, software for every conceivable application, and computer developments we haven't even thought of yet—will actually simplify our lives.

You can ask a dozen people whether or not any of these advances will make things simpler, and you'll get thirteen different answers. It's not an easy question, and I believe we each will have to answer it for ourselves. Some of us won't be able to move forward in our careers unless we're computer literate. Others will find limited computer applications for their lives. And still others will be dragged kicking and screaming into the computer age.

I recently conducted my own random and admittedly limited survey of a couple dozen acquaintances from around the country who are computer literate and who are active on the Internet. Even though they all agree that at the present moment the Internet has some sorting out to do before it actually becomes a useful tool for the average person, the consensus among all the people I spoke to was basically that, like it or not, the computer and Internet are here to stay, so we might as well get used to it.

Yes, perhaps. But the telephone is here to stay, too. And so is the television. That doesn't mean we have to allow them to take over our lives. For me, right now, a computer with a simple word processing program, a laser printer, and a fax are extremely helpful for my work as a writer. And I have no doubt that the Internet will someday soon prove to be a valuable reference tool.

But, knowing myself as I do, I will have to exercise a fair amount of discipline in my use of it, just as I do with television. I've already met a number of technocrats on the Internet who may never return to the real world.

Obviously that's their choice. (Or possibly not—there are addictive aspects to being on-line, similar to the addictive habits of sitting in front of a television screen, that we won't understand the effects of perhaps for some years to come).

But now that I've created a wonderfully simple life, I plan not to lose it to the Internet. We can keep abreast of the technology that is appropriate for our lives without losing our souls to it. All it takes is a clear vision of how we want our lives to be, and the discipline not to let them be overrun by so-called progress.

79. E-Mail

E-mail simplifies the mail and information handling for many of us.

But it can also complicate the process. I have a friend who uses E-mail exclusively now to keep in touch with her friends and business associates. It's so easy, she tells me. She can type a message, press a button, and send it to two hundred people in just a couple of minutes. And she does this now on a regular basis.

Yes, but she now spends several hours a day reading the return responses and then, in some cases, sending out another message. This is simple?

If you use E-mail a lot, you might take a quick moment to analyze how much more time you spend now dealing with the daily mail and various communications than you did before you incorporated E-mail into your life.

As one reader, Amy Newman, pointed out, "E-mail and voice mail were supposedly developed to make our lives simpler. This can be accomplished by responding immediately to 90 percent of all messages. E-mail should be responded to on-line, if possible, and should never be printed, responded to by hand, then retyped by yourself or an assistant—it amazes me how many people still do this. It takes practice to be confident enough to respond immediately, but it will save lots of time if you handle it on the spot."

E-mail is another convenience—just like the automatic washer and dryer—that is easy to overdo. It can complicate our lives precisely because it's so easy.

80. Automatic Payments

Gibbs and I reduced the complexity of our financial chores in a number of different ways, including closing out all but one bank account, eliminating all but a couple of credit cards, avoiding consumer debt, and consolidating our investment portfolio within just a couple of families of funds. And of course, our shopping moratorium (#56) has not only drastically decreased our spending but has also reduced the expenses we have to track.

After hearing from many readers that automatic payroll deposits and automatic payment withdrawals had greatly simplified their lives, I decided to explore those options.

It took a single phone call to set up the automatic payroll deposits. It took an hour or so to contact the companies I receive bills from each month—the mortgage, insurance, utilities, and so on. Each vendor mailed or faxed their own form requesting bank account information and our signatures so they could access our bank account for bill-paying purposes. It took a month or two to process this paperwork.

Now, payments for all but a few of the monthly bills are automatically deducted from our checking account. There are a couple of local utilities that are not, at this time, set up for automatic payments. Those I pay six months to a year in advance, so I only have to handle those bills once or twice a year.

The only check I write monthly is for the credit card bill, since at the present time the bank that services the card is not set up to utilize automatic payments.

The process of keeping track of the monthly charges is quite simple: I receive a statement each month from the utility companies, for example. Using the method of handling-it-only-once (#44), when the statement arrives in the mail I enter the amount that has been deducted from my checking account into my check register, which I keep at hand. At the end of the month I use the bank statement, which lists each automatic payment transaction, to reconcile the payments the bank made against the entries in the check register.

That's it. No check writing, no envelope addressing, no return addressing, no stamp licking, no having to get it into the mailbox on time. I've literally gone from spending a day or more each month on the bill-paying and record-keeping process to now spending little more than an hour each month.

One reason I hadn't pursued this avenue earlier was because I feared that by using automatic payments and deposits I'd lose control of the process. I imagined that deposits would get credited to someone else's account and that payments wouldn't get made by the bank, and then I'd have to spend hours straightening it all out. I clung too long to the belief that I could maintain better control if I was taking care of the payments myself each month. But I've been taking advantage of automatic payments and deposits for over a year now without a single glitch.

If there's any simpler way than this to pay bills, I'd love to hear about it.

81. Use a Monthly Spending Plan

O ne of the easiest ways I know to simplify your finances is to keep track of your monthly income and expenses so you can establish a workable spending plan to live within.

Numerous books are available today that will show you how to set up and maintain a budget. I describe several on the Reading List.

Or you can simply sit down and draw up your own system. I started years ago using a National Brand 14-column, double-page 11 x 8 1/2-inch analysis pad—available at any office supply store—to keep track of income and expenses.

It's quite simple. The various expense categories—mortgage, taxes, insurance, food, utilities, and so on, are set up vertically in the left-hand column; the months run across the top of the double-page spread.

At the end of the month I transfer the entries from our check register to the appropriate column in the budget book, total them, and deduct them from the monthly income.

At the end of the year, I total each expense for the year and divide by twelve to get the monthly average for each category. That number, adjusted up or down as needed, then becomes the budget figure for the coming year.

I keep this process very simple. This is not double-entry bookkeeping. It doesn't have to balance to the penny. In fact, to make it easier, I round up the numbers and never use the decimal point. It takes only a few minutes each month to total the columns and to keep up with the figures.

Tracking income and expenses makes it possible to increase your savings and control your spending, and it provides valuable information at the end of the year that can be used for the coming year's budgeting. It also greatly simplifies your tax records and reduces the time you have to spend gathering information for filing your tax return.

But probably the greatest advantage a spending plan offers is that it puts you in control of your money. Having that control will simplify your life.

82. The Simple Credit Card

When Gibbs and I were looking at ways to simplify our finances, we got rid of all but one or two of our credit cards. Not only did this drastically cut back on the hassle of keeping track of, rotating, and making payments on several different cards each month, but it cut back on the amount of junk mail we get each day.

Now that most grocery and department stores and even the U.S. Post Office accept credit cards, we use one card for all our routine monthly expenses such as groceries, gasoline, and any miscellaneous expenditures such as haircuts, personal items, office supplies, and so on. We keep a second card as a backup for traveling, since many hotels and car rental companies can tie up your available credit until your charges are finalized.

Since we know from our budget figures how much we spend in each category each month, it's easy to stay within our self-imposed limits. This way we don't have to carry excess cash around, which is more difficult to keep track of (and easier to slip through our fingers); and we don't have to carry a check-book—though we do keep a couple of checks on hand for the rare vendor that doesn't accept credit cards.

It's a simple matter to use the monthly credit card statement to record the entries into our budget ledger (#81), and every expenditure we can put on a credit card means one less check we have to reconcile with the monthly bank statement.

We found that it does take some discipline not to get carried away with credit card expenditures, and it's vital that you know the parameters of your budget so you don't go over your monthly limits. We make certain to pay the amount in full each month so there are no interest charges.

Using our credit card this way has greatly simplified the monthly record keeping. Now, all of our regular monthly bills are deducted from our checking account through automatic payments(#80), and most of the remaining expenditures are paid for by one check to the credit card company.

A debit card, available from your bank, is another simple way to take care of miscellaneous purchases and eliminates the need to carry extra cash. It works like a credit card, except the charge is deducted directly from your checking account. The charges are shown on your bank statement each month, and so can be reconciled and entered into your spending record as expenses.

A debit card eliminates the monthly check to the credit card company and of course there's never any possibility of interest charges for unpaid balances or late payments. Most banks don't charge for this service. If you use a debit card, be sure to enter each transaction in a check register just as though you were writing a check, and deduct it from your running balance. This makes it possible to keep track of expenditures as you go through the month.

83. Is Quicken Quicker?

A couple of years ago my accountant suggested that I could greatly simplify my annual tax preparation chore, as well as my monthly bill-paying process, by getting one of the mass-marketed computer bookkeeping programs that would automate these routines for me.

I consider myself to be moderately computer literate in terms of word processing systems, having used a variety of programs on various computers in the writing of my books.

But I hadn't gotten involved in computer bookkeeping systems because, even with my past involvement in real estate investing, most of the software available in those days seemed to be excessive for my needs. The fairly efficient bill-paying, budgeting, and end-of-year statements I did by hand were relatively easy and served my purpose well enough at that time.

But now that I'm simplifying, I'm always looking for easier approaches to time-consuming routines, so I decided to explore how the computer could simplify my life in this regard.

I spent roughly a hundred dollars on the software, checks, and envelopes, and a couple of hundred dollars on the consultant I hired to help me learn the program and to totally revamp my bill-paying methods.

After using the new system for roughly six months, I came to the conclusion that, for me, this is not simple. Since I don't keep the computer or the printer running when I'm not using them, it became far more trouble than it was worth to boot them up, replace the paper in the printer tray with computer checks, input the payment information into the program, print the check, pull out the computer envelopes, tear off the perforated checks, insert then into the envelopes, put a stamp on them, and drop them in the mail.

Now that all my monthly bills are handled by automatic payment through my bank, and I write only a couple of checks each month, using a computer program is overkill. Unless you're paying and tracking a significant volume of checks each month, now and even into the forseeable future, automatic payments are a much easier and less expensive way for the average household to simplify the bill-paying process.

Using a computer program for bill payments does, of course, eliminate the end-of-the-month number crunching, since the numbers are totaled instantaneously. And a computer program makes it possible to quickly analyze your income and expenses from many different angles.

If you've got a small in-home business and a significant number of bills to pay throughout the month, or if you have a complex tax picture, handling it all by computer would no doubt be simpler. But I accessed the system only once a month, so one consideration for me was the learning curve required to stay on top of it. In effect, I had to start all over again each month to get up to snuff with the program.

I also believe that, with the exception of monthly income and expense records, the charts, graphs, and reports that the software promoters tout as adding clarity to our financial picture are unnecessary for most of us. If you *want* those reports, or *enjoy* spending your time generating that type of data, that's one thing. But for those of us for whom that information is irrelevant, much of the advertising hoopla about the convenience of computer bookkeeping is overstated, at best. At worst, these programs can be far more complex than they appear.

No one can deny the incredible benefits computers offer us. And it seems possible that automated everything is just around the corner. But often, even with computers, we still need to evaluate objectively whether a particular application, or the way in which we utilize it, can really simplify or at least add something to our lives.

84. The Simple Time Management System

My system for time management parallels my system for keeping stuff organized. If we reduce the amount of stuff we allow to accumulate in our lives, we won't have to organize it. If we cut back on the number of things we have to do each day, we don't need a large double-page spread on which to track them.

If you take a close look at your system, you'll see that the things which are the most important aren't scheduled in there anyway. How many of us ever write in "Spend time with my kids today." Or "Take time for my soul this afternoon." Or "Have sex tonight."

Many people are finding a smaller date book is much more compatible with the simple life. As reader Melissa Keane wrote, "I moved out of my Filofax calendar with a full page per day because it led me to believe I could really *do* all that in one day. I'm a writer-historian-researcher, so most of my days can be filled with a one- to two-word notation: 'library,' 'archives,' or 'write.' I don't need hour-by-hour appointments noted."

The hectic lives we've created have become an acceptable and, in many circles, a respectable way to fill up complex and expensive time management systems. Have you ever added up how much time you spend keeping one of those systems up to date? Most of the time is spent *rewriting* on tomorrow's schedule the things you didn't get done today.

Getting to the point where we don't have dozens of things to do each day is a big part of what simplifying is all about. If you're thinking of going to a simpler system, it may take you several successively smaller sizes to get to simple. And obviously it will mean taking steps to cut back on the number of things you feel you have to do each day.

A hectic schedule is a lifestyle choice. We don't *have* to be chained to a huge time management system. As one proponent of the simple life, an executive from New York wrote, "I know I'm in trouble if I've got so many things to do that I have to make a list."

ELEVEN

Simple Parenting

85. Keep *Your* Life Simple

Simple parenting is an oxymoron, of course, since there are no simple kids. But our lives with our kids can be made simpler than they now are.

Simplifying with kids requires exactly the same things that simplifying without kids requires: time, energy, awareness of the problems, an understanding of the relevant issues, self-discipline, the ability to set boundaries (for both ourselves and our children), the strength of character to say no and stick to it, and the willingness to do whatever it takes to make the adjustments and rearrangements in our lives so we can bring about the desired changes.

The only difference is that simplifying with kids requires *more* of all this. Much more.

I want to point out that I don't have children of my own, though I do give myself some credit for marrying a man who has two terrific kids. Looking back, I see that simplified my life a good deal. They were 9 and 14 when I came on the scene, so I've never experienced the joy of changing a baby's diaper or the bliss of waking up for a 2 a.m. feeding (though I did share in a couple of sleepless nights with Gibbs when, at 2 a.m., it was clear our 16-year-old was not going to be home at midnight as we'd all agreed!).

Since the boys were with us only on the weekends and for vacations, I've never had to deal firsthand with the full-time, ongoing issues of laundry, chores, television watching, car pooling, day care, homework, drugs, teen sex, pregnancy, and the myriad other issues that full-time parents with kids face today.

But I've been surrounded my entire adult life with friends who have kids, so over the years I've observed some things that work and some things that don't work, and I have a couple of admittedly quite biased opinions of my own to share as well.

The best advice I, as a nonparent, can give to someone with children is this: Simplify your own life. In the process, the complications of having children will become more manageable.

If you could free up ten or twenty hours a week to spend with your kids or to eliminate or reduce some of the pressures you face—which simpifying will enable you to do— at the very least you can clear away enough of the day-to-day concerns so the dilemmas you have to deal with as a parent can be put in their proper perspective: Your kids are the most important issue of your life right now.

Continue to ask the question, "What do I need to do to simplify my life?" (#18). Just asking that question and taking the time to listen for the answer will provide you with the right solutions for your particular circumstances.

The suggestions that follow in this chapter are obviously not the only things parents can do to simplify their lives with kids. But, in terms of simplicity, they are, in my opinion, some of the most important ones to get started on.

86. Involve Your Kids in the Household Chores

Many parents wrote to say they had simplified their lives by requiring their children to help with routine household duties.

One mother, Jennifer Sellers, a secondary school teacher who has taken a sabbatical to be with her children, put it beautifully.

"This may seem like a no-brainer to anyone without children, but it is *rare* to find children who help with household chores today.

"I was at a talk given by John Rosemond, who writes about parenthood, and he asked the audience, 'How many of you have children over five who have regularly assigned chores that must be done to certain standards—and they don't get paid to do them?'

"In a full auditorium only half a dozen hands went up.

"He then asked how many of those present had chores when they were kids. Every hand went up. 'That's one generation, folks,' he responded.

"My children do a lot willingly and for no monetary pay. We achieve this by:

1. Letting them 'help' when they were little. It would actually take me twice as long to accomplish the task with this 'help,' but it gave me time to talk with my children, and the task eventually did get accomplished. The payoff is that now I have excellently trained assistants who truly do help today.

2. Use working together as an opportunity to be together. When you've finished playing Candyland, your work still waits. When you've made soup together, you've gotten dinner accomplished, trained a future cook, visited together, and your child will blossom from the pride of making dinner.

3. Being profuse with thanks and gratitude and compliments and comments.

4. I've found it's better to give young children several short chores rather than one long task. My youngest wipes off the cat's mat and the trash can lid, takes out the recycling and compost,

washes the compost bucket, wipes off the counter where the re-cycling piles up, and changes the kitchen linens daily.

All of these are things I used to do and don't do now. None in themselves are time consuming, but collectively they save me time and energy and don't overwhelm my 7-year-old. He dries dishes every third night (three children), but I don't ask him to wash the evening dishes. I feel it would be too much for him and stifle his desire to help.

My teenagers do longer tasks. Sometimes I pay them to help, but only for a special usually strenuous task, never for a regular chore.

5. I stress how lucky they are to be learning how to do things and how to work. They'll be the ones getting the jobs in the future.

"I always try to remember that a child's self-esteem is not built by silly stickers that say, 'You are special!' but rather by having achieved a genuine sense of accomplishment and a sense of being a contributing and valuable member of the community (family)."

A friend of mine who has three children simplifies the household chores by posting a chart of duties on the fridge door each month. If there's any question about whose turn it is to do the dishes, for example, she can point to the chart as the authority. This eliminates any discussion. (She does end up with a fair amount of graffiti on the chart, however.).

87. Curtail Their Extracurricular Activities

I hear from both parents and kids on this one. And it's heartening to learn that people are starting to figure out that even though *everything* is available to kids today, kids don't have to *do* everything.

One mother of two teenage children wrote to say they had finally sat down together as a family and made a group decision: only one or two extracurricular activities per season per kid.

Both parents were surprised at first at how readily the kids agreed to this seeming restriction. But as time went on, they found that not only were the kids amenable to the idea of fewer after-school activities, they were actually relieved at the prospect of not having to compete and/or perform in so many different areas: dance, golf, gymnastics, hockey, and voice lessons for her; football, hockey, track, and chess for him.

Over the course of the two years since they began this cutback, they've all become aware of the following benefits.

The kids are no longer exhausted from being constantly on the go. Their mother is relieved of the responsibility of being on call as the family chauffeur. Both kids' academic performance has improved dramatically and so has their performance in their chosen activity.

They get along better with each other and with their two younger siblings. The mother's private explanation for this is that they all now have more of her time, so their innate need to compete for her attention has diminished.

The family as a whole is happier because they're less stressed out and each has more quiet time on their own.

We've been so imbued in recent years with the belief that we have to take advantage of all the opportunities out there. The urge to *do everything* complicates our lives. We've lost the ability to distinguish between the things we'd like to do and the things we feel we should be doing.

We've passed this complication on to our kids. Often we allow peer pressure—our peers and our children's peers—to influence our decisions. We want our kids to have the same opportunities that all the other kids have, or opportunities we didn't have. But it's so easy to get carried away. We don't have to do it all. Our kids don't either.

You could start by cutting back on even one or two after-school activities to see if it doesn't greatly simplify your lives.

88. Monitor Your Children's Television Viewing

In psychologist John Rosemond's excellent book, *Six-Point Plan for Raising Happy, Healthy Children*, he makes a strong case for heavily monitoring what our children are watching on television.

The fact that much of the television programming for kids—not to mention for adults—is of questionable value is not at issue here; though the quality of the material available should be sufficient reason for any caring parent to curtail television usage.

According to Dr. Rosemond, even programs like *Sesame Street* and other socially acceptable educational kids' shows foster passive learning traits that are detrimental to a child's future learning abilities.

But there are other issues here that are not often addressed. We think allowing a child to sit in front of the television screen simplifies our lives because it gives us a break. But according to

Dr. Rosemond, not only does regular television viewing stifle initiative and creativity, but it develops addictive patterns and children who depend on you, rather than on themselves, for their entertainment. Children who grow up not knowing how to create their own happiness and sense of well-being are going to be entering the real world with a major handicap.

And any child who has developed the ability to think and do for himself or herself is going to have a decided advantage over all those developmentally impaired kids who spent an average of seven hours a day in front of the tube.

Because of the harmful effects of television on a child's ability to learn, Dr. Rosemond believes no child should be allowed to watch television until they've learned to read well. Then, if permitted at all, television should be closely monitored and greatly curtailed.

Set parameters. They can watch an hour a day of a program you approve of. And perhaps another hour of a quality educational program. Then the set gets turned off. My friend Vera bought a television with a hidden control switch, so the set can't be turned on in her absence.

Pick up a copy of Steven and Ruth Bennet's *365 TV-Free Activities You Can Do with Your Child*.

If you need some outside support in eliminating television, contact TV-Free America, 1322 18th Street NW, Suite #300, Washington, DC 20036 (202) 887-0436 for a free booklet that will show you how to organize and participate in a TV-free week in your community.

89. Teach Your Kids How to Handle Money at an Early Age

When I was 8 years old, my dad started giving me an allowance of fifty cents a week. The only advice he gave me at the time was to save half of it. I could do whatever I wanted with the other half, but it was to take care of any extras I might want. If I spent it all in one place, which I did for the first couple of weeks (all twenty-five cents of it), I couldn't go running back to Dad for more. I had to wait until the next weekly infusion of cash. I learned pretty quickly how to set aside money for unexpected contingencies—the double feature *and* popcorn on Saturday mornings—and how to budget my income.

This allowance was not connected to any household chores I was required to participate in. I had long been expected to do basic tasks like making my bed, helping set the table for dinner, and hanging up my clothes after school.

My involvement in chores increased as I got older; they were what I was expected to contribute as a member of the household. My allowance was my parents' way of getting me accustomed to handling money wisely. They provided all of my basic needs, but expected me to budget for and pay for any extras I might want.

By the time I entered high school I had my own checking account and a savings account and knew how to reconcile them both. Thanks to Dad's guidance, and his willingness to let me fall on my face a couple of times, I grew up confident about my ability to handle money so I could always take care of my basic needs and have money left over. The habit of saving part of my income has stayed with me through all my working years.

Mary Hunt, in her book *The Cheapskate Monthly*, outlines a similar program she and her husband used to get themselves out of debt and to set up their two boys with a program for handling their own expenses at an early age.

There are a couple basic differences in her program and my dad's. The first is that each child was required to save 10 percent and also to give away 10 percent of their income to a cause of their choice. It could be to a needy friend, to the local library fund, or to a charity.

Secondly, they gave the boys a larger amount of money, which was to cover *everything* above the basic room and board provided by the parents. And they gave them a raise at the beginning of each school year that was appropriate to the expenses each child would be encountering. So the boys had to learn to budget for *all* their expenses, including clothes, school books, entertainment, school trips, bus money, birthday gifts for friends, family presents, and everything else.

The parents agreed not to interfere with how the kids spent their money. But they made it clear that the boys couldn't come to them for more money if they spent it all early in the month and needed more to get them through. If they ran out before the next "payday," that was tough; they'd just have to wait.

While Mary admits it was hard to refuse her kids the extra money they thought they needed when they spent it all on the first day, they stood by their rule.

As a result, both boys quickly learned how to handle money

at an early age. By the time the boys were old enough to drive, they each paid for their own cars—and the gas and insurance needed to run them—and also had money set aside for continuing their education.

Mary's book lists some guidelines in terms of the amount of money that would be appropriate for various age groups. Any of her principles could be adapted to your children and your own circumstances.

For example, not every child is mature enough to be trusted with a month's allowance. If you have a child who would spend it all on candy (or beer, or drugs), you'd need to dole the money out more carefully and perhaps require a strict and detailed accounting of how the money is spent.

Teaching your kids how to handle money wisely will not only simplify your life, it could be one of the most powerful gifts you give them.

90. Set Buying Limits for Toys and Candy and Stick to Them

One of the more publicly visible complications that parents have with children is played out in supermarket checkout lines across the country week after week. It's the chilling scream of the distraught child whose mother has not yet agreed to allow him to purchase both the gummi bears and the space cadet suckers.

One solution is to leave the kids at home when you go shopping. Obviously, there are times when it's not possible to do this. And besides, kids need to be taught how to behave in public. So in one sense, grocery shopping is a good training ground.

I've discussed this with dozens of parents, and they all agree the answer seems so simple: Just say no. But the trick is to say no or let your kids know what you will allow them to buy, if anything, *before* you go into the store, and then stick to that decision.

Describe ahead of time what the consequences will be if they cry or throw a tantrum, and stick to that, too.

Another approach is to start as early as possible to use an appropriate variation of Mary Hunt's allowance system (#89), and, within reason, let each child learn to make his or her own decisions about how to spend the money they have available.

91. Set Limits for Your Parents and Other Well-Intentioned Relatives, Too

It's one thing to set parameters for items you buy for your kids or what you allow them to purchase, but it's just as important to set the parameters for what your parents and grandparents can buy for your kids.

For years, my friend Liz has purchased extravagant Christmas gifts for her niece and nephew who live several thousand miles away from her. Several years ago she had an unavoidable business trip that took her out of the country for most of December. Since she was going to be away over the holidays, she made her gift selections early and sent them off to her sister at the end of November.

She called several days later, just before she was to leave the country, to wish them all Merry Christmas and was shocked to find out that the kids had already opened her presents.

"But why didn't you wait until Christmas?" she wailed to her sister.

"Liz, they get so many presents from the grandparents and the stepgrandparents and the aunts and uncles and other assorted family members that if they don't open a package or two each night, starting several weeks before Christmas, they'd still be opening presents halfway through January."

This sounds like a situation that's gotten out of control. But it's not all that unusual. Not only does this excess of gift giving complicate the parents' lives because of all the toys, games, and other paraphernalia that are taking up space in their home, but it complicates the children's lives as well. It becomes overwhelming. They don't know what to play with first. It numbs their sensitivity and their creativity.

If you're watching, you'll see that invariably they pick one or two toys that become their favorites, and the rest sit idly, taking up room and cluttering up their space.

It also sets up unrealistic expectations that can never be fulfilled in the real world. And it certainly gives them a negative message in terms of consumerism and the habits of responding to television advertising (100 percent of the ten best-selling toys are tied to television shows).

You might want to start setting some parameters for your parents—the kids' grandparents—as well as aunts and uncles and friends and relatives. "Look, Mom, we appreciate all the things you do for the boys, but we feel we need to set some limits on the number of toys that come into the house and complicate our lives. We'd like to limit the number of presents to one or two, and any other money you want to spend will go into a college fund."

It's that simple.

92. Cultivate Simple Values

Relaxing on some of the household chores; reducing your social commitments; cutting back to eight-hour workdays if you are employed outside the home; reducing your commute time; spending less time shopping and consuming; changing your expectations about the size of your house, the green of your lawn, and the whiteness of your laundry will make it possible for you to create the time to teach your kids simple, mind-expanding, soul-filling activities.

In addition to teaching them to cook and sew and do their own laundry as Jennifer Sellers has done (#86), try taking them on nature walks and bike rides, and teaching them to use the public library and spend quiet time there. Plant a garden, build castles in the sand or castles in the air, watch sunsets and sunrises. Teach them to seek out quiet time each day and to enjoy developing their own inner resources as appropriate to their age, through reading, writing, journal writing, and their own creativity through music, drawing, painting, and any other artistic leanings they might have.

As reader Ann Hopson wrote, "As the parent of two young children, I feel lucky to have found this avenue to explore. My girls, 5 and 7, love nature, new experiences, and freedom, so your suggestions are a happy alternative to Chuck E Cheese, amusement parks, and costly mall shopping. We love visiting free places like botanical gardens, local historical sites and museums, and even doing genealogical studies in libraries, which have become our family's favorite resource. Luckily, my girls are happily entertained at home with our own simplistic activities."

Yes, these activities will take more of your time, certainly in the beginning, than sitting them in front of the television. But in the long run, having happy children who love simple pleasures and who can be their own source for entertainment will make life simpler for you and for them.

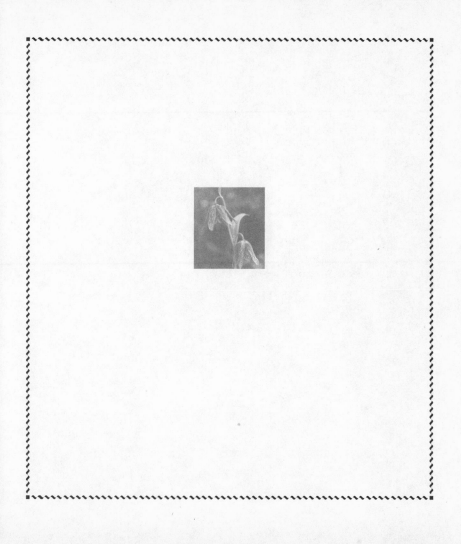

TWELVE

Simple Wardrobe Ideas for Women

93. Make Your Own Rules

I gave a talk on simplifying recently and when it came to the subject of simple clothing, the women in the group were commiserating on how difficult it is to deal with the vagaries of women's fashion. Many of us are fed up with the herculean task of putting together a suitable look that is functional and versatile and doesn't cost an arm and a leg.

One of the men in the audience announced that he was an investment banker who puts together venture capital for the fashion industry. He said the women's clothing designers and manufacturers were going through some very tough times and a lot of restructuring because sales have been down considerably in recent years, far more than the overall downturn in the economy would explain.

He was hearing over and over again that women were tired of struggling with the frustration of trying to find clothes that worked for them. He said the feeling in many parts of the industry was that women had simply stopped buying clothes the way they used to. As he saw it, the entire fashion industry was going to have to make some drastic changes in the way they designed and produced clothes for our rapidly changing lifestyles.

I hope he's right. But it would be surprising to see any monumental changes in the promulgation of fashion trends in our lifetime. Clothing designers and manufacturers have spent too many billions of dollars creating the epidemic feelings of discontent in American women. It would be a major turnaround for them to suddenly start producing clothing that actually works for the majority of women.

If you've reached a point in your pursuit of the simple life where you can move to that cabin in the woods or in some other way arrange your life so you can ignore even the minimum decrees of the fashion industry, you can probably limit yourself to a couple of sets of jeans and a pair of boots—which is my ultimate ideal—and get away with it.

But those of us who plan to remain in the swing of commerce—either by choice or by circumstance—will probably continue to play the fashion game to one degree or another. The objective, as far as I'm concerned, is to set as many of my own rules as I can, and to play the rest of them as simply as possible.

There are many women out there who feel as I do about this issue. We're not interested in being fashion plates, but we want or need to look presentable, and we'd like to do so with the least amount of fuss, bother, and expense.

Needless to say, it'd be a lot easier if we could just say to hell with Madison Avenue and ignore the incredibly powerful dictates of the fashion industry. If you've been able to do that, congratulations. You're ahead of the game.

I haven't yet reached the point where I can disregard all those edicts, but, with some effort, I have gotten to a point where I can turn my back on a lot of them.

After some months of pondering this issue I finally put together a simple look that works for me. And I learned a few things in the process.

I discovered that when it comes to clothes—as with many other things—less is definitely more. It's so much simpler to work with a few classic pieces that are always in style and work with each other than to have a closet jammed with the latest fashions that, if they ever look good, don't look good for long and seldom work together.

I figured out that I don't need a multitude of colors in my closet. I've greatly reduced the complexity of putting together a suitable look by limiting my palette to two or three basic colors that are always in style.

I see no reason to have more than a few pairs of shoes in my closet at any one time. And they all have the same heel height.

I've eliminated the accessories that have cluttered up my drawers for years, most of them seldom used.

I've found the simplicity of a couple of pairs of earrings liberating beyond belief.

I've learned to make certain that every piece of clothing I buy has pockets so I don't have to carry a purse.

I built a simple wardrobe around a couple of outfits that I already had in my closet and I liked. I wanted one basic look that I could use as a uniform, which I could layer to take me through the seasons.

One of my challenges was to find out why these particular outfits worked for me, so I could easily add to them through the years as one piece wore out, and so I could repeat the process when I needed to (which I hope won't have to be any time soon).

I know many women would not be happy with the limited range of colors and styles this approach embraces. But if you're looking to create your own simple look, I hope there will be some principles here that you can adapt to your own set of rules, based on your own needs and circumstances, rather than on the whims of fashion.

94. Start with What You Already Have

One of the rules we used to get rid of the clutter in our home was "If you haven't used it in a year, throw it out." The first place we started with was our closets.

I was strongly tempted, when I looked into my closet and saw all the things I hadn't worn in over a year—some for many years—to throw out everything but the clothes on my back and start over from scratch.

Though I got rid of a lot of stuff on that first attempt, I didn't quite have the nerve to get rid of everything. Later, I was awfully glad I hadn't.

It turned out that, mixed in with all the clothes I hadn't worn recently—and with a lot of things I had worn but wasn't crazy about—there were several treasures. These were outfits—a couple of jackets, a long skirt, a pair of slacks, some simple tops—that I'd had for a number of years that I quite liked and I had continued to wear over and over again.

I wore them so much because I always felt good in them. They were comfortable. The colors, the style, the fabric, and the look all suited me. So I kept them and got rid of most, though at this point, not all, of the other clothes—the sweaters, suits, blouses, shirts, jackets, shoes, boots, and several drawers of accessories that I knew I'd never wear again.

Those few pieces I liked became the starting point for my new simplified wardrobe and stayed in the front part of my closet. There were other items that I wasn't sure about, which I hung in the back of the closet as a safety net, just in case my ideas for my simple look didn't pan out. Eventually, as my new wardrobe took shape, I felt more comfortable about letting go of the fall-back pieces altogether.

If it feels as though your closet is out of control and you've been thinking you'd like to take some steps to simplify it, start slowly, and don't jettison *everything* just yet. The chances are good that you, too, have some old favorites that you wear over and over again. If so, keep them.

If you know why you like them and why they work for you,

the job of building from them (or replacing them with similiar pieces if need be) will be much easier. But if, as I didn't, you don't have a clue why they work, don't worry about that part just yet. There is help available. But you might find it useful to sort through a couple of other questions first.

95. Limit Your Color Scheme

A few years back I had my colors done by one of the color consultants that were in vogue at the time. I came away from that session with a two-foot-square display board that I could hang in my closet, to which was attached at least four dozen color swatches, representing all the different shades of colors that would be suitable for my skin tones.

I was also given a credit card–size, accordian-type, color-swatch holder containing these same colors, which I could conveniently keep in my purse so I could stay within my range of colors when I went clothes shopping. You probably know the type of color charts I mean.

When I started weeding clothes out of my closet in my first attempt to simplify my wardrobe, it dawned on me that just because this consultant said I *could* wear all these different colors, it didn't mean I *had* to. I didn't have all those colors in my closet of course, but it felt like I did.

In theory, each color in one's palette could be worn with every other color in one's palette. But in my experience, it never quite worked out that way. I've always suspected that all the clothing manufacturers got together and conspired to make sure that none of their colors worked with the palettes the color consultants were working with.

But if they don't do that, there's no doubt that many of them go to great lengths to figure out how to formulate this year's "in" colors so that, not only do they not work with last year's "in" colors, but they don't work with any previous year's "in" colors either. Though those color palettes are now somewhat passé, many women still buy clothes with their color charts in mind.

The result is that millions of us have ended up season after season with numerous outfits in our closets, no one piece of which ever blends with any other piece. It's just one of the many ways clothing manufacturers lure us into starting all over again each year in our seldom attainable attempt to create an acceptable fashion statement.

I began to see that having such a wide range of colors was a major complication for my wardrobe. So I narrowed my palette down to three colors.

The colors I chose, black, white, and shades of gray—with complements of taupe—would not be everyone's choices and, in fact, I'm not certain they're my first choices. I decided on these colors because my favorite outfits—the ones I wore over and over again, and that I always felt good in, and were therefore the ones I wanted to build my simple wardrobe from—were in these colors.

Also, I stayed with these mostly darker colors because, as several readers with the same idea pointed out, darker colors are easier to work with from season to season and lend an aura of quality and professionalism to your total look.

(Since my simple puppies are black and white and gray, I figured I could simplify the dog hair issue at the same time: The black hairs would end up on the black clothes, the white hairs would end up on the white clothes, the gray hairs would end up on the gray clothes, and, as we all know, taupe goes with everything. It doesn't quite work out that way, but if I alter my expectations slightly, I can overlook the dog hair.)

I don't feel I have to stick with these colors for the rest of my life, but they work for me now and into the forseeable future. And with basic colors like these, I can always add a splash of color in a vest or a top to put a bit of zip into my palette from one year to the next should I feel so inclined.

Limiting your palette also simplifies your accessories—your jewelry, scarves, belts, purses, and shoes.

Take a moment right now to imagine how much simpler shopping for clothes would be if you limited yourself to three or four of the colors that look best on you. Just think of the tremendous number of clothes you could pass right by because they don't fit into your color scheme.

96. Figure Out Your Clothing Needs

For years I had hoped to find one classic all-purpose outfit that would be suitable for my work life, my social life, my exercise regimen, and every other possible event.

I would then acquire seven copies of that magic outfit—one for each day of the week as Einstein reportedly did—and that would be it. I'd never again, well, almost never again, have to bother with the task of building a suitable wardrobe or with spending time each day figuring out what to wear.

It's possible my life will one day be so simple that one outfit will work for everything I do. But I've finally figured out that for now I need clothes for at least three separate circumstances: casual clothes for my morning walks and for my day-to-day work at the computer in my home office; business attire; and something in between—not dressy but not sweats—for wearing into town for a luncheon meeting or for a casual dinner out.

Since we simplified our lives, formal attire has become a non-issue. On the rare occasion I attend a formal gathering, one of my business suits has to do. Otherwise, as Thoreau did, I tend to avoid events that require fancy garb.

If you don't already know what they are, it might be helpful to take some time to figure out the kinds of clothes you actually need for the types of activities you engage in.

This seems so obvious, but I see this mismatching of form to function over and over again. I know many women, for example, who love business suits and who therefore have a closet full of them, but whose work life actually calls for more casual attire. They have a closet full of clothes and nothing to wear.

97. Find Your Best Silhouette

The factor that moves the subject of fashion up a couple of notches on the complexity scale is the tremendous variety of styles that are available for women. Men's fashion options are fairly limited and predictable. But the possibilities for women know no bounds. Consequently, it's a tremendous challenge for most of us to find an acceptable style, or silhouette, that works for our particular body type.

Pulling together a suitable silhouette seems like it should be easy. But how many times have you gone clothes shopping and fallen in love with an outfit because it looked terrific on a mannequin, or even on the hanger, only to get home and find it doesn't look all that great on you.

You love the fabric, you love the color, you love the idea of it, it's exactly the type of thing you think you need. But even though you tried it on in the dressing room, the fact is it simply doesn't work.

More likely than not you keep it because it's just too much trouble to take it back and start all over again. Then it's guaranteed to be one of those outfits that ends up in the back of your closet that you never wear or is not comfortable when you do wear it.

Often the reason it doesn't work is that, even though it may fit size-wise, it doesn't fit silhouette-wise. It's either too long in the waist, or too short in the length, or too narrow in the shoulders, or too broad in the hips, or too frilly, or too severe, or *something* else is wrong with it.

Whether you're short or tall, large or small, young or old, broad or narrow, there is at least one silhouette that can make you look and feel like a million bucks. *Finding* it may not be simple—though it can be done—but *having* it will be.

Zeroing in on one or two silhouettes that work for you will simplify your present and future wardrobe immeasurably. Once you find a look you're comfortable with, you can build on it forever. You can add a piece one year and drop a piece the next year, or fill in pieces as you need them. You can dress it up or down. Using layers, you can take it from season to season.

Finding one of your ideal silhouettes will eliminate the continual frustration of never being satisfied with how you look. It will make it possible for you to get up in the morning, get dressed, and not have to think about clothes for the rest of the day. It'll save you time. It'll save you money. It'll be one less thing to complicate your life.

You may already know what silhouettes suit you best. But if the prospect of figuring it out has always been one of life's great mysteries, you can simplify the process by getting some help.

98. If You Need Help, Get It

After struggling with the problem of trying to figure out what clothes work for me and why, I finally decided to bite the bullet and get some help.

My plan was to find a salesperson in one of our local stores who had put together a good look for herself and who would be able to help me do the same.

Over a couple of weeks, I spoke with three or four different women in various clothing departments, outlining what I was looking for. The first two made some halfhearted attempts to help, but were obviously not all that interested.

The third young woman was enthusiastic but, after I saw what she had pulled together from the racks, it was clear that she didn't have a clue what she was doing for me, even though she had quite a good look for herself.

On the fourth try in as many weeks I hit the jackpot. I found a woman who was enthusiastic and knowledgeable, and clearly understood what I was trying to do in creating a simple look. Very briefly I outlined what I was looking for in terms of my various clothing needs and the colors I wanted to work with.

We set up an appointment for later in the week—to give her some time to pull some possibilities together—and she asked me to bring in the outfits that I liked from my own wardrobe so we could build from them.

Maryke spent several hours with me over the next couple of weeks. She showed me what worked from my closet and from the clothing she had selected from the racks and what didn't and why—either a jacket was too short, or a skirt too long, or the cut wasn't right for my shape, for example.

With her help I was able to zero in on the best silhouette for my body type. She helped me add a couple of pieces to my existing business outfits and to find a comfortable, washable, work-at-home look that, with some easy layering, I can use year round. And we added a couple of other pieces that dress down the business look or dress up the casual look so I can greatly expand the serviceability of each piece in my closet.

Building a simple wardrobe with the help of a personal shopper has made it possible for me to reduce my clothes shopping excursions to once a year, or less. It's been over a year and a half, and the only new items I've acquired are some T-shirts to take me through the summer.

Now that I understand my silhouette and know what pieces I need to make it work for me, I can avoid the impulse shopping which contributes to corporate profits but seldom does anything positive for my wardrobe.

Getting some professional advice saved me an incredible amount of time, energy, and money, and it has immeasurably simplified my life.

If you can't find a knowledgeable salesperson to help you, perhaps you have a friend who has an innate sense of style who can steer you in the right direction. Or you may be able to find a personal shopper listed in the yellow pages. Or simply ask around for the name of someone who can guide you once you carefully explain your parameters. Just remember to keep in touch with your own intuition through the process.

And don't overlook consignment shops as an excellent source of quality clothing for your simple wardrobe.

99. The Simple Purse

One day several years ago I pulled into the parking lot of my neighborhood grocery store. As I was getting out of the car to go in to do my shopping, I happened to look over at the car that had pulled in beside me.

I watched a woman get out of the car, sling her duffle bag–sized purse over her shoulder, and walk across the lot into the store.

I knew for a fact that she was going to spend the next twenty minutes or so walking around the store with that bag over her shoulder. She'd come to the checkout counter, pay for her groceries, bring everything out to the car, climb in, and drive off.

She would have spent all that time carrying that huge bag around with her, and the only thing she would use from it would be a check or a two-inch by three-inch plastic credit card that weighs a fraction of an ounce.

I knew this because it was exactly the same thing I was going to do, and exactly what I had been doing for years.

I went home that night and emptied the contents of my bag onto the dining table. I sorted through every item and pulled out only the things I had actually used during the past week: my wallet, a pen, my lipstick, and a huge ring of keys. I put everything else back in the big bag, and found a smaller bag to hold the items I had actually used.

I put the large bag in the trunk of my car, in case I might actually need a pair of packaged rain slippers, a serrated knife, a small bottle of hand cream, a slightly shredded package of tissues, an empty perfume atomizer, a large hairbrush, a slightly mangled miniature tube of toothpaste, a small flashlight, a handheld calculator, or any of the other vital accoutrements we tuck away in those gargantuan totes.

Six months went by. The emergency supplies in the trunk of the car went untouched. The strap-shaped crease in my right shoulder gradually faded. It occurred to me that I could possibly pare down some more.

I went through the same exercise with the smaller bag. What

had I used from that bag recently? Four plastic credit card–sized cards: my driver's license, my library card, one credit card, and a triple A card—which I hadn't actually used, but you never know.

I pulled the money out of my wallet and set aside the wallet, with all its miscellaneous photos, old receipts, mangled business cards, and tattered pieces of paper with cryptic notes. I folded the green money, along with a couple of checks, and put these with the plastic cards. I ringed them all with a wide rubber band on which, just for the heck of it, I wrote "Gucci" in black ink.

I got rid of all the keys except a single car key, for which I don't need a ring. (I use a garage door opener to get into my house.) Since I seldom write checks anymore (#80), I don't require a pen—though there's always one attached to a counter with a plastic cord should the need arise.

I had already stopped wearing sunglasses because it had become such a hassle to change them back and forth and to find them in the bottom of my bag.

I keep any spare change I might pick up from a folded money transaction in the car's ashtray.

I keep a small emergency supply of tissues in the glove compartment.

Eventually, I got rid of the emergency bag from the trunk of the car.

I will say that even though I was delighted to be free of having to carry a heavy bag around all the time, I did go through some withdrawal pangs. Not only had I been in the habit of having a purse with me for many years—so for a brief time I felt almost *undressed* without it; but it had also become my security blanket. There lingered the small nagging concern that I might *need* one of those mostly useless items I had always carried with me. But, having seen all those items strewn over the dining table, I knew that I hadn't actually used any of that stuff for a very long time, in some cases, ever.

It didn't take long to get comfortable without a purse. Once I began to experience the freedom of not having to deal with that huge bag of stuff, there was no going back to carrying a handbag.

So now, in the pocket of whatever I happen to be wearing, I keep my "Gucci" rubber-banded cards/check/folded green stuff, my car key, and the one thing I would need above all else should I ever be stranded on a deserted island, my lipstick.

That's it. It's so simple. It's so liberating.

THIRTEEN

Simple Wardrobe Ideas for Men

100. Gibbs's Ideas for Simple Clothes for Men

Gibbs has volunteered to share his own thoughts about simple clothes for men. Here they are:

"When it comes to business clothing, men have it a lot easier than women. Unless they're actors, they need only look neat, clean, and like everyone else they work with. The simple fact men's clothing manufacturers would like you to forget is this: Nobody notices what a man is wearing unless it's weird.

"Years ago, a friend of mine simplified his business wardrobe by restricting it to one gray suit with two pairs of pants, three blue shirts, one tie, one pair of shoes, and several identical pairs of socks. Nobody noticed.

"I asked him if there was anything he'd do differently. He said next time he'd get a suit with three pairs of pants, because pants wear out much faster than jackets.

"Clothing that isn't for work can be chosen mostly for its function—fishing, woodchopping, ballroom dancing, for example. Pick it primarily for how well it does the job.

"As far as appearance is concerned, just don't buy anything that glitters."

There's probably not a whole lot more that needs to be said about simple clothes for men. That in itself says a lot.

A FINAL THOUGHT

It's been more than five years since Gibbs and I first made the decision to begin living simpler lives. Looking back, we see it as one of the better decisions we've made. Not only has it been a fun and challenging adventure, but it's given us the incredible opportunity to step back and take life a little less seriously. We've come to see that even though we'll never get to do it all, we can still be happy and fulfilled. In truth, it's more often than not the quiet, simple moments that bring depth and meaning to our lives.

At its most basic level, the process of simplifying allows us to cut back on the incredible number of time- and energy-consuming options that confront us every day.

It was only a few years ago that when you wanted an ice cream cone, you could choose vanilla, chocolate, or strawberry. Now there are dozens of flavors to choose from. It was only a few years ago that when you wanted a new car, there were only a couple of dozen models to choose from. Now there are hundreds of models to choose from. You can apply this same expansion of options to nearly every area of our lives: the food we eat, the clothes we wear, the television programs we watch, the music we listen to, the sports we participate in, the web sites we frequent, and so on.

It's gotten to the point for many of us that taking the time to consider all the flavors takes away a good portion of the time we have to enjoy the ice cream. As reader Kathy Louv said, "I'm learning to take the Baskin-Robbins out of my life."

How do we do that? We start by becoming aware that the problem exists. Then we train ourselves to minimize the number of options we get exposed to through the clutter we accumulate, the activities we participate in, the expectations we try to meet, and our excursions through the mall.

But of course, having no options can complicate our lives, too. One of the greatest challenges we all face is to find a happy balance between the opportunities that are available to us, the media-implanted urge to have them all, and our own desire to keep focused on the things that really matter.

READING LIST

Household/Family

Campbell, Jeff. *Clutter Control: Putting Your Home on a Diet.* New York: Dell
   Trade Paperback, 1992. Dozens of books on the market tell you how
   to get organized. In my opinion this is one of the best. It's a basic,
   no-nonsense approach. It's also a great companion book to *Speed
   Cleaning*, listed next. But remember, the best way to control clutter is
   to get rid of it, and keep rid of it. That's one of the basic tenets of
   the simple life.

Campbell, Jeff, and the Clean Team. *Speed Cleaning.* New York: Dell Trade
   Paperback, 1987. A delightfully easy system for simplifying household cleaning chores.

Rosemond, John. *Six-Point Plan for Raising Happy, Healthy Children.* Kansas
   City: Andrews and McMeel, 1989. Paperback. Outlines a simple, basic

approach to raising children who are responsible and depend on themselves for their entertainment and, ultimately, their happiness. Also spells out Rosemond's guidelines for family television use.

Wilson, Mimi, and Mary Beth Lagerborg. *Once-a-Month Cooking*. New York: St. Martin's Press, 1986. Paperback. Describes a step-by-step plan for preparing two weeks or a whole month of main-meal dishes at a time.

Work/Creativity

Boldt, Laurence G. *How to Find the Work You Love*. New York: Penguin, 1996. This book won't give you the answers but it will guide you to the right questions. It explains beautifully why, for your own growth and peace of mind, you have the duty and responsibility to find your life's work.

Cameron, Julia. *The Artist's Way: A Spiritual Path to Higher Creativity*. Los Angeles: Jeremy P. Tarcher, 1992. Paperback. Following the steps outlined in this book may help you find the work you love.

Orsborn, Carol. *Enough Is Enough: Exploding the Myth of Having It All*. New York: Putnam, 1986. A delightfully readable story of one superwoman's decision to start living with a saner scale of expectations.

Saltzman, Amy. *Downshifting: Reinventing Success on a Slower Track*. New York: HarperCollins, 1991. A business journalist's look at how our attitudes toward work and leisure are changing for the better. Outlines five strategies for downshifting. Includes interviews with people who've made the decision to lead more balanced lives and tells how they did it.

Schor, Juliet B. *The Overworked American: The Unexpected Decline of Leisure.* New York: Basic Books, 1991. A scholarly documentation showing how the demands of employers and the addictive nature of consumption tie us to longer work schedules and reduced leisure time. A real eye-opener regarding our present-day work habits.

Money

Dacyczyn, Amy. *Tightwad Gazette II.* New York: Villard Books, 1995. Paperback. This book, along with Dacyczyn's first book, *Tightwad Gazette*, lists hundreds of ways to spend less money. These books embrace and celebrate frugality, and offer many practical, thought-provoking, upbeat, and amusing discussions on saving money that everyone can use.

Dominguez, Joe, and Vicki Robin. *Your Money or Your Life: Transforming Your Relationship with Money and Achieving Financial Independence.* New York: Viking, 1993. Paperback. This book will change the way you think about money and offers a practical plan for simplifying both your financial life and your work life. Shows how to set up a monthly budget and how to use a graph for keeping track of income and expenses.

The Green Group. *101 Ways to Save Money and Save our Planet*. New Orleans: Paper Chase Press, 1992. Paperback. The emphasis in this little book is on saving money through sensible practices that are good for the planet.

Hunt, Mary. *The Cheapskate Monthly Money Makeover*. New York: St. Martin's Press, 1995. Offers a palatable approach for reorganizing your financial life and for developing a healthy attitude about money. Also outlines a workable system for establishing a monthly spending plan.

Long, Charles. *How to Survive Without a Salary*. Toronto: Warwick Publishing Group, 1991. Paperback. Some interesting ideas on how to get along with less and make do with what you have. Not a lifestyle that will necessarily work for everyone, but it shows what's possible.

Terhorst, Paul. *Cashing in on the American Dream: How to Retire at 35*. New York: Bantam, 1990. Written by a CPA and a former partner at Peat Marwick Mitchell & Co. who cashed in and retired at 35. Assumes you have equity either in your home or stocks that you can put to work for supporting an early retirement. The numbers and rates of return he cites aren't realistic in today's financial climate, but if you have the equity available, his plan can be adapted to other circumstances.

Lifestyle

Bennet, Steven, and Ruth Bennet. *365 TV-Free Activities You Can Do with Your Child.* Holbrook, MA: Bob Adams Publishing, 1991. Paperback. Includes both indoor and outdoor activities that require little or no preparation and that will provide hours of entertainment which otherwise might be spent in front of the television.

Eisenson, Marc, Nancy Castleman, and March Ross. *Stop Junk Mail Forever.* 1994. Available from Good Advice Press, Box 78, Elizaville, NY 12523 (914) 758-1400. $3. The best program I've come across for eliminating junk mail.

Kelly, Jack and Marcia. *Sanctuaries.* Bell Tower, 1994. A guide to monasteries and retreat houses. Published in both an East Coast and a West Coast edition.

Lindbergh, Anne Morrow. *Gift from the Sea.* New York: Vintage Books, 1978. Another perspective on simple living and what complicates our lives.

Peace Pilgram: *Her Life and Work in Her Own Words.* Available from Ocean Tree Books, Post Office Box 1295, Santa Fe, New Mexico 87504. Paperback, 1992. This is the incredible story of a woman who simplified her life down to a comb and a nail file, and then carried a message of love and peace around the country. Anyone who longs for a truly simple life will love this book.

Simple Living Journal. Available from Publisher Janet Luhrs, 2319 North 45th Street, Box 149, Seattle, WA 98103 (206) 464-4800. $14 per year (U. S.). This is a quarterly newsletter that shares ideas about simplifying and tells personal stories of people from around the country who are doing it.

Stoll, Clifford. Silicon Snake Oil: Second Thoughts on the Information Highway. New York: Doubleday, 1995. A fascinating look at computers and the hype surrounding the Internet, written by a computer expert. A witty and perceptive explanation about how and why computers can both simplify and complicate our lives.

REFERENCES

Mail Preference Service, P. O. Box 9008, Farmingdale, NY 22735-9008. Write and request that your name and any variation of your name not be sold to mailing list companies. This is a first step in the process of reducing the amount of junk mail you receive. Many other effective steps you can take are outlined in *Stop Junk Mail Forever*, listed above.

National Association of Professional Organizers, 1033 La Posada Drive, Austin, TX 78752 (512) 206-0151. With over 700 members around the country, this association may be able to help you locate a professional organizer in your area to help you get rid of the clutter in your life.

Real Goods Trading Corporation, 555 Leslie Street, Ukiah, CA 95482 (800) 762-7325. Source for laundry disks and other environmentally friendly household products.

TV-Free America, 1322 18th Street, NW #300, Washington, DC 20036 (202) 887-0436. This national nonprofit organization was founded to raise awareness about the harmful effects of excessive television watching. They will send you a free booklet that will help you organize a TV-free week in your community.

UNPLUG, 360 Grand Avenue, #385, Oakland, CA 94610 (510) 268-1100. If Channel One with its heavy commercial loading is in the schools in your area, contact UNPLUG for information about what you can do to keep your schools commercial free and to limit your child's media-induced wants.